THE NEHEMIAH PRINCIPLE:
A CALL TO LITERARY EVANGELISM

By Sharon C. Jenkins

ISBN: 978-1-7354642-8-2

Printed in the United States of America

Sunshine Reigns Publishing Company (A subsidiary of The Master Communicator's Writing Services)

Houston, Texas

www.mcwritingservices.com

TABLE OF CONTENTS

FOREWORD

৪০০৪

Since my childhood, when my mom read And to Think That I Saw It on Mulberry Street (the first Dr. Seuss book), I've loved books. In high school, my English teacher David Smith saw potential with my writing and encouraged me to join the newspaper staff. As I wrote sports (even as a non-sports person), I learned the rudimentary skills of writing a story. I continued writing and during my senior year was the editor of that newspaper. I decided to study journalism at Indiana University, one of the top journalism schools in the U.S. From my high school experience, I thought I was a solid writer and joined their student newspaper staff. I rewrote my first story several times and when it appeared (without my name), it was about three paragraphs. It taught me I had a lot to learn about the writing profession.

I went to college in the pre-computer days and we wrote our stories on a royal typewriter. While raised in the church, college gave me a new-found freedom and I rebelled from the church. Indiana had about 30,000 students on the Bloomington campus. I joined a social fraternity and spent time writing my newspaper stories and at times skipping class.

Early one morning I was at the newspaper writing my story and on deadline. We were seated shoulder to shoulder next to another desk and another student who was also writing their story. Because of the previous night activities, I could not get my fingers on the right keys. Back then when you made a mistake, you simply backed up, x-ed out the error and kept typing. My story was full of xxx's and I knew my editor would be complaining. With each mistake, I muttered to myself, "Jesus Christ."

Finally the blonde –haired girl, Nancy, next to me said, "Terry, don't say that because one of these days when you really need Jesus, you will call out for him and he will not be there." I wondered what she was talking about since I thought I was a Christian. I was someone in the pew at church but I had no personal relationship with Jesus. Nancy recommended I go to a little Logos bookstore a couple of blocks off the campus and look at their cards and posters. Maybe I would find a book there too.

A couple of days later, I wandered into the Christian bookstore and bought a book called Jesus, the Revolutionary. I wondered, "How could Jesus be a revolutionary?" As I read the pages, I learned about a side of Jesus that I had never seen. Jesus was not just a figure praying in the garden or someone blessing children. Jesus was real.

About this time, someone invited me to attend a group of Jesus people meeting in an old warehouse. As I sat on those pieces of carpet with the candles, I could see those people had something that I didn't have—a personal relationship with Jesus. I changed my life direction and ever since December 1972, I have been walking the Jesus trail.

I'm sure my journalism classmates thought I had lost focus or something because of my career change. Instead of going to some major newspaper after graduation, I joined Wycliffe Bible Translators and spent 17 years with them—10 of those years in linguistics. I worked among the Southwest Cakchiquel people in Guatemala and nationals completed the translation of the New Testament in August 1990.

When I returned to my writing, I started writing for Christian magazines. It's where I recommend any new writer begin the journey because of the exposure, training and much more. I understand people want to write books but you can learn a great deal in the magazine area.

As of today, I've written for more than 50 magazines and I've written more than 60 books. God has provided some incredible writing opportunities for me. I'm grateful and know the printed word changes lives. We know the Bible changes people's lives but books and magazine articles also change lives. I know first-hand because a book changed my life. In recent years, I've worked with hundreds of authors through three different book publishers as an editor plus a short stint as a literary agent. As an acquisitions editor I'm the first person to read their material and see if it something Morgan James Publishing will publish. We receive over 5,000 submissions a year and only publish about 150 books and only about 25-30 of those books are Christian.

The world is full of opportunity for every Christian writer. With The Nehemiah Principle, you have a remarkable resource. Sharon Jenkins is the Master Communicator and knows the challenges and opportunities in publishing. I recommend you study this book and take action on the principles here. It will open incredible doors of opportunity for your own life and writing.

W. Terry Whalin
Thewritinglife.ws
Terrywhalin.com
@terrywhalin

INTRODUCTION

ɛɔɲ

So God told you to write a book, so now what?

Sometimes when we hear the call, it's nice to have an instruction manual to guide you through to the end of your manuscript. Whether you are writing for ministry or to make money to finance your God project, knowing where to start and how to get equipped for the journey is imperative to your end result. *Christian AUTHORSHIP: Mastering the Business of Writing* is the answer to your prayers. It is one of the few books which address the Nehemiah Principle for writers.

The Nehemiah Principle equips aspiring Christian authors for their marketplace ministry "for such a time as this." Christian authors are called by God to write for the glory of His kingdom. Being a Christian writer is more than conforming to the world's standards for writing success it is accepting the Macedonia Call for writers. You must be available, ready, and able to write a message which has global impact and be in a position to see the message gets to its targeted audience are crucial proponents of The Macedonian Call. Let's refresh your mind as to the events surrounding Paul and Timothy's call to ministry in Macedonia.

> *The Macedonian Call*
> *And they went through the region of Phrygia and Galatia, having been forbidden by the Holy Spirit to speak the word in Asia. And when they had come up to Mysia, they attempted to go into Bithynia, but the Spirit of Jesus did not allow them. So, passing by Mysia, they went down to Troas. And a vision appeared to Paul in the night: a man of Macedonia was standing there, urging him and saying, "Come over to Macedonia and help us." And when Paul had seen the vision, immediately we sought to go on into Macedonia, concluding that God had called us to preach the gospel to them. Acts 16:6-10 (ESV)*

Knowing you are called is one thing, but knowing where you are called is another. Paul and Timothy knew without a doubt God called them to fulfill the Great Commission. It was Jesus' last commandment He left the apostles before His ascension. As writers we too must ask God, where is He sending us with our tablets, laptops, or MacBook's.

Accepting Him as our Lord and Savior was the beginning of the process of our total surrender to God and His will for our lives. Everything He has endued us with is for the glory of His kingdom. The question is how will you glorify God with the gift of authorship?

This is where the Nehemiah Principle comes into the picture. Once you have accepted the call, there is a season of preparation to fulfill it. The "call to write," is as serious a call as that of an apostle, preacher, or teacher. Nehemiah was called to the palace as the king's cupbearer. He had a very important position, he was trusted with the very life of the king. There wasn't a day that went by he wasn't in his presence. Obviously the king and Nehemiah had a mutual respect for each other, so much so he was moved to investigate his sad demeanor. When Nehemiah shared his heartfelt sorrow for the state of his homeland, the king was moved with compassion to help him resolve the problem. Not only did Nehemiah accurately articulate the problem but he had a suggested solution for the king that incorporated his assistance. His relationship with the king opened his heart to help fulfill the restoration of God's temple.

Nehemiah did not go before the king without first going before God. Like Paul in the Macedonia Call, he did not move until he got clear instructions from God. Then and only then was he ready to address the king. Nehemiah's prayed the following petition to His God:

> *The Prayer of Nehemiah*
> *And I said, "O Lord God of heaven, the great and*
> *awesome God who keeps covenant and steadfast love*

with those who love him and keep his commandments, let your ear be attentive and your eyes open, to hear the prayer of your servant that I now pray before you day and night for the people of Israel your servants, confessing the sins of the people of Israel, which we have sinned against you. Even I and my father's house have sinned. We have acted very corruptly against you and have not kept the commandments, the statutes, and the rules that you commanded your servant Moses. Remember the word that you commanded your servant Moses, saying, 'If you are unfaithful, I will scatter you among the peoples, but if you return to me and keep my commandments and do them, though your outcasts are in the uttermost parts of heaven, from there I will gather them and bring them to the place that I have chosen, to make my name dwell there.' They are your servants and your people, whom you have redeemed by your great power and by your strong hand. O Lord, let your ear be attentive to the prayer of your servant, and to the prayer of your servants who delight to fear your name, and give success to your servant today, and grant him mercy in the sight of this man."
Nehemiah 1:5 – 11a

Christian writers choose authorship because they are moved to minister, evangelize, share their message, want to solve a BIG problem or have a desire to make money to finance kingdom projects. The Holy Spirit prompts you to use your gifts and callings to bring hope to a crumbling world just like He did Nehemiah. He was moved by the sad state of affairs in his homeland enough to do something about it. There are numerous reasons for Christian writers to be compelled to share the Gospel in today's world. God wants you to become a part of the solution. That's the purpose of this book, to empower you to fulfill your Macedonia Call to write using the wisdom Nehemiah used when he was rebuilding the wall of Jerusalem.

This book equips readers to effectively take care of the spiritual and business side of writing while consecutively building content which will equip, edify, course correct, and exhort their reading audience through the love of Christ. Each chapter ends with an activity and a prayer which reinforces the Nehemiah Principle discussed.

Christian AUTHORSHIP keeps you mission focused on your purpose driven writing project and addresses such topics as time management, financing your book project, discovering your publishing personality, and how to write with a God resolve in mind. This book was specifically designed for Christian authors who desire excellence in their writing ministry while embracing their marketplace assignment to handle the business side of writing throughout the life of their book project or writing career.

The Mandate

Can a Christian writer be a tool for Kingdom building with their pen? Absolutely! As the prophets, psalmists, and apostles wrote the living word of God, so must you. If you are a Christian and have been commissioned for service by Jesus, then you must surrender your pen to that purpose. Let's take a look at the Great Commission:

> "Then the eleven disciples went to Galilee, to the mountain where Jesus had told them to go. When they saw him, they worshiped him; but some doubted. Then Jesus came to them and said, "All authority in heaven and on earth has been given to me. Therefore go and make disciples of all nations, baptizing them in the name of the Father and of the Son and of the Holy Spirit, and teaching them to obey everything I have commanded you. And surely I am with you always, to the very end of the age." (Matthew 28:16 – 20 NIV)

The qualifiers are:

a. You must first be a disciple of Jesus,
b. Have an ear to hear Jesus' voice and a heart to follow Him,
c. Accept your authority in Him,
d. Be willing to equip others to serve Him,
e. Maintain a continuous relationship with Christ forever.

If you notice, Christ does the equipping. When Jesus called the apostles, they were common men with ordinary skills. They were not the elite or recognized religious leaders of their time but men and women who witnessed and experienced His love and were enamored by its limitless power. Love drew them, captured them, compelled them, and kept them in the faith.

So shall it be with you. You have the unique responsibility of bringing the written testimonies of His glorious love to the modern day electronic parchment of our age and do it in His authority. Informing, educating, and inspiring others to walk in the fullness of their calling.

Being Equipped for the Call of the Pen

The "Call of the Pen" is not a 21st Century concept. From the beginning of time men have been chronicling the acts of God and man's relationship with Him. As Christian authors, called according to God's purpose, whether it's to give testament of His personality, share present-day miracles, envelope our readers in the joy of the Lord, or fulfill our calling to compel mankind to follow Christ, we must be equipped to do so. If you are called to the marketplace ministry of being a writer as a career, you still have the mandate of serving your clients, readership, and those who are in positions of authority over you in excellence. Just as if God was peering over your shoulder, making sure you were completing a heavenly task.

That's where AUTHORSHIP comes into play. Traditionally writers and authors have followed the dictates of the literary industry and often got lost on the designated professional pathways which defined career success, but these pathways may not have lent themselves to a righteous cause or fostered the call God had on their lives for ministry in the marketplace. Historically, the plans of man have often been in conflict with the will of God. True success is embedded in the dictates of a righteous God who desires your success in life more than anything else. Jeremiah 29:11

states, "For I know the plans I have for you," declares the Lord, 'plans to prosper you and not to harm you, plans to give you hope and a future.'" So the main premise throughout this book is God's unchangeable plan for your success and equipping you for the "Call of the Pen," whether it's in ministry or the marketplace.

How Does AUTHORSHIP Fit Into the Picture?

Discipleship is defined by Merriam Webster as "one who accepts and assists in spreading the doctrines of another." As a disciple of Christ you are a living example of His doctrine and everything you do represents His excellence. Being equipped for your modern day calling as an author requires you be permeated with all that is Christ. You were born selected to fulfill your call and are required to surrender to the training process. Mastering your craft may require you be a lifelong learner.

Over the last twenty years we have seen the literary industry experience a major paradigm shift that totally shook up the status-quo. Believe it or not, God was not surprised. Being the Alpha and Omega, nothing catches Him by surprise. Just like He had a remnant of believers when Elijah had his breakdown after he battled Jezebel (1 Kings 19), he has a training program for the 21st Century author. It's called AUTHORSHIP!

The path to authorship is a long one, but it is not unpaved. As I mentioned earlier, there are many examples of authors in the Bible. To survive in today's market, we have to adapt to be Authorpreneurs. Do not be discouraged — the Bible has a model to follow for the business side of writing. In the book of

Nehemiah, we can see a business model for Christian authors that will withstand both the good and bad times ahead. Be encouraged and grab your pen for the glory of God's kingdom. The benefits are heavenly!

CHAPTER ONE

THE NEHEMIAH PRINCIPLE

ഇ൦ൠ

THE TWELVE TENETS OF CHRISTIAN AUTHORSHIP

Nehemiah was a man on a mission. He was also a man of prayer. Once he heard Jerusalem was in distress, he went before God: repented for his nation and his family and asked God for a plan for restoration. His name means "Jehovah comforts." He was truly a comfort to Judah in a city surrounded by their enemies, the Samaritans, Ammonites, Arabs, and Philistines. His response to the blatant opposition was "I am doing a great work. How can I come down?"

It only took him 52 days to build the temple but he stayed in Jerusalem as the Governor of Persian Judea for 12 years before returning to Susa and King Artaxerxes. While in office he focused on repopulating Jerusalem, purifying the Jewish community, and returning them to the law of Moses He also enforced Jubilee (the cancellation of debt) and had the Jewish men who were married to non-Jewish wives divorce them. His focus was on returning the heart of the people back to their God. In doing so he used the following twelve Christian leadership tenets to anchor his foundational belief system while doing the work of the Lord.

CHRISTIAN AUTHORSHIP TENET ONE
Nehemiah had a heart for God!
Have A Heart for God
Love the Father Enough to Be Moved By What Moves Him

CHRISTIAN AUTHORSHIP TENET TWO
Nehemiah was moved with compassion for God's people.
Be Moved With Compassion
Let Love Be Your Aim

CHRISTIAN AUTHORSHIP TENET THREE
Nehemiah accurately identified the problem that needed to be solved.
Identify A Problem
Let Your Pen Address a Specific Need or Passion

CHRISTIAN AUTHORSHIP TENET FOUR
Nehemiah sought God for a solution.
Develop A Solution
Partner with the Holy Spirit for a Literary God Solution

CHRISTIAN AUTHORSHIP TENET FIVE
Nehemiah solicited King Artaxerxes for the help he needed.
Enlist Help
Develop a Publishing Team that Makes Your God Dream Work

CHRISTIAN AUTHORSHIP TENET SIX
When Nehemiah arrived on the scene, his first course of action
was to evaluate the problem.
Evaluate The Problem
Do Your Research

CHRISTIAN AUTHORSHIP TENET SEVEN
Nehemiah went about implementing his plan to rebuild the
city wall.
Implement Your Plan
Write that Manuscript

CHRISTIAN AUTHORSHIP TENET EIGHT
Nehemiah stayed focused on the plan at hand and kept the
people focused.
Stay Mission Focused
Beware of Enticing Propositions

CHRISTIAN AUTHORSHIP TENET NINE
Nehemiah was prepared to fight his enemies within and those
on the outside of the wall. *The*
Fight If Necessary
Be Prepared for Writer's Block, The Enemy Within

CHRISTIAN AUTHORSHIP TENET TEN
Nehemiah was purpose driven.
Stay The Course
Be Tenacious in Adhering to Your Writing Schedule

CHRISTIAN AUTHORSHIP TENET ELEVEN
Nehemiah threw a grand celebration when the wall was finished.
Celebrate The Victory
There's Nothing Like Holding Your Book Baby in Your Hand

CHRISTIAN AUTHORSHIP TENET TWELVE
Nehemiah returned to evaluate the progress of the people after the job was completed.
Evaluate Your Results
Don't Rest on Your Laurels, Your Work Has Just Began

Being a Christian author is a ministry. When you accept the calling to use your pen for His glory, it may require some spiritual alignment, but if you use these twelve tenets to build your Christian AUTHORSHIP writing ministry, you will do a great work for the kingdom of God. May He remember you for your good! (Nehemiah 13:31)

> *So Ezra the scribe stood on a platform of wood which they had made for the purpose... An Ezra opened the book in the sight of all the people, for he was standing above all the people; and when he opened it, all the people stood up. And Ezra blessed the Lord, the Great God. ~ Nehemiah 8:4 – 6*

Somewhere around 538 – 457 B.C., the priest and scribe Ezra came on the scene after the people of Judah were released from Babylonian captivity. All 42,360 of them returned to Jerusalem and restored worship in the city and rebuilt the temple of God. They too were confronted with opposition from neighboring tribes but persevered because God was with them. King Artaxerxes gave Ezra full authority to return to Judah because they were in need of a priest and someone who was well versed in the law of God.

Imagine a broken people who once knew the great wealth of Solomon returning to their homeland after 70 years of being exiled. Strangers in their own land and strangers to their religion. Just as the children of Israel had wandered around the desert for 40 years, they were slaves in a foreign land for 70 years unable to serve their God and worship Him in spirit and in truth because of their sin, but God had mercy on his people and turned King Cyrus' and King Artaxerxes hearts to please Him and his children had favor with both of them and sent them Ezra and Nehemiah to bring healing to their nation.

The Old Testament Scribe

Ezra was a scribe and a priest. In this chapter, we will take a closer look at his God mission. The word "scribe" or "sopherim" in Hebrew has three meanings – (a) to write, (b) to set in order, and (c) to count. In essence, a scribe was a king's administrative assistant, writing letters, transcribing old records or drawing up decrees and managing his financial records.

In the kingdom of Israel, they were leaders entrusted with the transmission of religious, historical, and legal documents. Without them fulfilling their roles as copyists and interpreters there would be no Bible.

CHAPTER TWO

THE MODERN DAY SCRIBE

⅏⅏

During the days of Ezra, a scribes' role gained a significant degree of importance because they were responsible for restoring the sacred books, laws, hymns, and the words of the old prophets. They recorded the Old Testament and held one of the most important and sacred duties of "recording the very words of God through the men who were inspired by the Spirit of God to write what God intended for them to write."[1] Ezra is called, "a ready scribe in the law of Moses" by his New Testament peers (Ezra 7:6), "a scribe of the words of the commandments of the LORD, and of his statues to Israel" (Ezra 7:11), and "the scribe of the law of the God of heaven" (Ezra 7:21). Ezra was the scribes of all scribes because he "had prepared his heart to

---

1   http://www.patheos.com/blogs/chritiancrier/2015/07/22/who-were-the-scribes-in-the-bible-a-christian-study/

seek the law of the LORD, do it, and teach Israel statues and judgments." (Ezra 7:10)

Some scribes were also lawyers, philosophers, teachers, and councilors who stood beside the priests. They also wore the title of "rabbi" and rendered a large number of rulings and legal interpretations in Rabbinic literature.

Other Old Testament References to Scribes: Jeremiah 8:8, Esther 8:9, 2Kings 12:10, 2Kings 25:19.

The New Testament Scribe

During the New Testament period of time, the scribes came from priests, Levites, or commoners who were learned teachers and influential leaders. In the New Testament they were highly regarded officials, advisors to the high priests, teachers of the law of Moses, experts on Judaism and leaders in the community. Jesus told the people scribes had been sent by God to encourage the people to repent.

We saw evidence of their impact throughout the gospels (Matthew 7:29, 15:1-6, 23:16 – 23). Unfortunately, they were on the wrong side of Jesus' mission. Wrapped in their manmade knowledge and the traditions of men and thinking more highly of themselves than they ought, they did not even recognize the Messiah. Scribes had authority in the Jewish community because they had knowledge but instead of using it to bring the people to Christ, they used it to maintain their powerful positions in the church.

The Modern Day Scribe

Scribe - writer; specifically: journalist. [2]

A few years ago I took a part-time job as a scribe writing notes for college students with disabilities. Often when we think of a modern day scribe, we think of someone who takes notes. It wasn't until I did a biblical study on the word itself that I gained a greater understanding of the true meaning of the word in reference to my responsibility as a Christian writer. Like the New Testament scribes, we are of the spiritual make-up and status of Ezra in the eyes of God. The level of our responsibility and accountability equates that of a biblical teacher. In James 3:1, the scripture admonishes us to be cautious about accepting the call of a scribe/teacher. It specifically states, "Not many of you should become teachers, my fellow believers, because you know that we who teach will be judged more strictly." (NIV) Scribes have the heart of the people in their hands, therefore; they must tread circumspectly when communicating God's word. You may say, "Well I'm not a preacher, teacher, or prophet, I just write Christian fiction." It's the spirit of truth that is reflected in your book which changes lives, renews minds, and fixes broken hearts. The qualifying factor for Christian writers to be scribes for Jesus is simply their accepting the call to write for the glory of His kingdom, the kingdom that has no end.

Let's take another look at Ezra. Earlier we shared that the scriptures say Ezra was the scribes of all scribes because he "had prepared

---

2   www.merriam-webster.com/dictionary/scribe

his heart to seek the law of the LORD, and to do it, and to teach Israel statues and judgments." (Ezra 7:10) As you can see here preparing your heart for ministry has a lot to do with the quality of your service. In the New Testament scribes were prone to be motivated by their peers, the people, popularity, or their position when writing or teaching God's word. They strayed from God's truth to the point they didn't even recognize the Messiah and He was right in their midst. He walked, talked, and ate with them, but they were so bound up in tradition and the ways of man they missed the true purpose of His ministry. When you consider the impact Jesus had on the world during His brief 33 years on earth, imagine what it would have been like if the scribes of His time were a part of His ministry.

Yet, God gave the children of Israel numerous times to get it right. We have the benefit of the lessons they learned because of the scribes in the Old and New Testament. We have a divine opportunity to fulfill the call of God on our lives to be writers for Jesus. The world needs us now more than ever to be Jesus' arms extended with our pens in hand ready for service. You have the powerful backing of the Holy Spirit, our helper, to change the face of a nation, one chapter at a time. Don't waste it on personal and professional pursuits that don't line up with God's call on your life. "But seek first his kingdom and his righteousness, and all these things will be given to you as well." (Matthew 6:33)

CHAPTER THREE

MASTERING AUTHORSHIP

୫୭ଠଏ

Mastering What?

AUTHORSHIP: Inquiring Minds Want to Know

As a writer, your personal "why" is unique. You might write primarily for ministry, financial compensation, or just because writing is in your DNA. Perhaps your passion for your message will not let you walk away from the blank page. I often get lost in the passion of writing ignoring the practical business elements. What stands in the gap between passionate writer and published author? Sometimes, it's mastering the art of AUTHORSHIP.

What is AUTHORSHIP?

To properly understand the word "AUTHORSHIP," we must look at the two words that lend value to our definition: "author" and "entrepreneur." Lying on my desk is this huge red book titled,

Webster's New World College Dictionary. I could have visited Google, but I am an old library junkie and the rustling of crisp pages makes me smile.

Webster's definitions:

Author: a person who makes or originates something; creator; originator. They are a writer of a book, article, blog, etc. An author is a person whose profession is writing books.

Entrepreneur: a person who organizes and manages a business undertaking, assuming the risk for the sake of the profit.

My definition:

AUTHORSHIP: the business of authoring, marketing and publishing your work. You actively participate in the planning, implementation and evaluation of the process to create your book, eBook, blog, editorial, white paper or article and its distribution as a partner or independent publisher. If you are a Christian, it includes placing Christ at the center of your marketplace calling to write for the glory of His kingdom.

Inquiring minds want to know what "AUTHORSHIP" really is. First, let me tell you what it's not. It's not selling books out of the back of your car, keeping them packed in boxes in the garage, or selling a few to families and friends. Even though some national best-selling authors such as Wayne Dyer, John Grisham, and Lynn Harris started out that way today's author has so many other alternatives. If this economy has you thinking out of the box and you are looking for ways to increase your book sales, then you will want to master the art of AUTHORSHIP.

The extent of your involvement in the process is determined by whether you are self-published or published by a traditional publisher. A self-published author often practices AUTHORSHIP because they organize and manage the content creation, publishing, marketing, sales and distribution of their end product. As a self-published author, you are more in control of the overall management of the book writing process, publishing, and distribution process, therefore; mastering AUTHORSHIP is critical to your continued success as a writer.

If you have a contract with a publishing house, your exposure to AUTHORSHIP will be quite different. The publisher will take on the responsibility for some of the elements in the AUTHORSHIP process and you will form a partnership to successfully complete the process.

Writing is serious business! When you sit down with pen in hand, if you are writing for ministry, you must begin with the end product in mind. "If I write it, they will come" is not the best philosophy for a writer in a troubled economy. If you are writing for ministry, money, or need money to write, you must have a plan of action that will get you there.

Often writers simply turn the business side of their trade over to the "experts, "such as virtual assistants, ghostwriters, print-on-demand publishers, etc. Experts cost money. Prudent business owners desire to get the best value for their investment. It has been my unfortunate experience if you don't do your research to identify their credibility then you may end up assuming a loss. On the other hand, the "do it yourself route" can cripple your chances of success if you are not well versed in AUTHORSHIP. Whether you choose the "do it yourself" route or pay for help, you can still achieve your objective, but you first must master the art of AUTHORSHIP.

Authors often want that the book contract that will fulfill their "bestseller" dreams, but the industry is changing as rapidly as technology is changing. The traditional Christian publishing houses are being more discerning when selecting authors because they are in the business of publishing to make money. It's not impossible to break into the industry but it does help if you have mastered your craft. Publishing houses more readily sign seasoned writers with a reputation for good writing and those that possess a following.

Writing is like any other profession or ministry. If you want to be at the top of your game, you must prepare. Preparation and perspiration are repeatedly the best tools associated with small businesses mastering their businesses. It's no different in the writing industry.

Self-publishing is now an acceptable alternative. As a result, the market is being flooded with self-published authors because the opportunity is available to anyone who desires to publish a book. There's nothing like seeing your name in lights on a new book cover and establishing yourself as an expert on a particular topic.

The story doesn't change with the entrance of traditional publishers. They are the industry midwives that lend their expertise and capital to the success of your book. Nevertheless, once the editors, graphic designers and publisher, etc. finish with the book, the burden frequently falls on the author to assist in the marketing and promotion of the book. There is no easy way around it because no matter how well developed a book is, it is only as successful as the author's ability to get it into the hands of the reader. This is why mastering the art of AUTHORSHIP is imperative. Aspiring authors must learn what publishers already know. This is a business and it means nothing to have a book published if no one picks it up to read it. Luke 14:28 – 30 states, "Suppose one of you wants to build a tower. Won't you first sit down and estimate the cost to see if you have enough money to complete it? For if you lay the foundation and are not able to finish it, everyone who sees it will ridicule you, saying, 'This person began to build and wasn't able to finish.'" Count the cost of the investment you are making into God's kingdom so that you will be able to finish and make God proud of the work that you have done to fulfill His will on the earth.

I remember the first time I saw my name on a self-published book cover. I was on a self-induced high for a week and then the real work began. Since then, I've had the privilege of coaching several aspiring authors. It has been my goal to ensure their success from beginning to end. I now feel the need to expand my reach so more authors can experience success. Regardless of where you find yourself in the AUTHORSHIP cycle this book is designed with you in mind. Happy Writing!

If I write it, they will come ... or Not

After a gut wrenching two years of laboring with *Beyond the Closet Door and Christ's Rescue from Abuse*, I was spent. It is my own personal story and I had to revisit some life events I'd put to rest a long time ago. My motivation was to help adults who were victims of child abuse accept the provision for them won at Calvary. I'd found a POD publisher to print the book and also expected them to market it. Contribute it to my naivete as an author, but I expected tons of people to be so intrigued with my story they would buy cases of it to share with victims of abuse everywhere in the world. NOT SO. I didn't have a clue about marketing, distribution, or my target market. Frankly, I gave away more books than I ever sold. I now offer it at the extremely low price of 99 cents on Amazon Kindle as a ministry outreach and that's the happy ending of that story. These days the results would be quite different because I have a black belt in AUTHORSHIP.

Are you a dreamer or a doer?

Passion has fueled a great number of writer's pens and there is nothing wrong with that. Sometimes, it is just about writing your story and sharing it with the ones you love. In other words, it's okay to dream about writing a book. I personally, have written numerous fiction stories in my head over the years. One day, one of those characters is going to escape and I will be on the trail to perfecting my craft in another genre'. Perhaps you are a 'griot' that has been entrusted with the stories of your ancestors and dream of the day you will put pen to paper to document your family's history. It's all good, but in the words of my grandmother, "Nothing comes to a dreamer, but a dream."

Everything begins with a dream or a vision, but dreams don't accomplish a thing until those ideas are put into action. In short, dreamers must become doers.

A 'doer' does something with the intent of an expected outcome or reward.

What does your expectancy look like in regard to your current book project? Do you want to be a best-selling author? Do you envy the mastery of Stephen King or King David in the Book of Psalms?

Whatever your passion identify it early in the process. Then take the following steps:

◈ Do your homework. Is your book dream a pipe dream or is it something that can be implemented and bring value to you and others? Will people pay for it? If so how much?

◈ Have realistic expectations. For example: Ask yourself and others is it realistic to expect to sell 1 Million e-books in 5 months without doing some kind of research on your target market or building a fan base that which fosters that kind of growth especially if you are not into social media.

◈ Let your moral compass be your guide. It is critical when you are establishing your reputation as a writer to set appropriate boundaries which are an accurate representation of who you are and your belief system.

Study the habits of authors on the best-seller lists. Reach out to your favorite authors and build relationships with them. I read Michelle Stimson's *Boaz Brown* and fell in love with her writing style and contacted her by e-mail. To my surprise, she emailed me back and we have been friends ever since. When I did my first book signing in Dallas, she was there. In the early days, I learned the value of reaching out to successful authors and building relationships with them. As a result, if I am stuck in the middle of an AUTHORSHIP decision, I can call several of them to get valuable advice.

Summary

AUTHORSHIP focuses on mastering the business side of writing. It's a process if applied correctly, can reap benefits beyond your expectations. If you are mission or ministry minded AUTHORSHIP is for you. The tools discussed in the chapters that follow were designed to assist you in maximizing your investment. I am reminded of the Parable of the Talents (Matthew 25:14 – 30) as told by Jesus in the Bible, the amount of time and energy invested into reaping a harvest dictated the sower's return. So roll up your sleeves and let's get busy taking care of your business and expect fabulous things to happen as a result. It's okay to dream big. It gives you something to reach for. Especially if you are reaching big for God!

CHOOSE YOUR PUBLISHING MODEL
– SELF PUBLISHING OR TRADITIONAL
PUBLISHING OR HYBRID PUBLISHING

There are two lucrative but very different approaches to publishing. Which one is right for you? As a coach, I am frequently asked this question. Historically there has been more prestige attributed to being published by a traditional publishing house. With the onset of electronic publishing, self-publishing has become a viable alternative. I've known authors who have equal appreciation for both methods.

One of my favorite authors, Linda Hudson Smith, has been traditionally published for most of her career and I had the opportunity to sit and listen to the glamorous tales of her past book tours and signings with stars in my eyes. I have known many authors who have waited for "the deal" with a traditional publisher because that's what they were most passionate about. On the other hand, most of the authors I have coached are interested in self-publishing because they want more control over their book. You have an opportunity to make an informed decision about what's best for you. It's important to understand there are challenges to conquer in all of the publishing models. Your mission is to choose the one best for you, just like David did when it came to fighting Goliath. He used what he knew worked for Him before, a slingshot and some pebbles. He could not use Saul's armor to fight Goliath because it did not fit him. You may not be able to use the publishing model your favorite author or friend has used because God didn't design it to be used by you to accomplish the task He's called you to do. Seek Him for the publishing method best suited for you through prayer. He is waiting to answer that question; all you need to do is ask.

Decisions, Decisions, Decisions

Let's take an analytical approach to the two different methods of publishing: traditional publishing and self-publishing.

The Traditional Publisher

The aspiring author completes their manuscript and sends a query letter or proposal to a traditional publisher. The details for submission are usually outlined by most traditional publishers on their website, including if an agent is required. If the author has an agent, they will do this for them. An agent acts as an intermediary for the author and most traditional publishers require submission through an agent. An agent will send your manuscript out to several publishers he or she thinks is a good fit for your project.

Once a publisher receives your work, an acquisitions editor will review the manuscript to determine if it is a good fit for the publishing company and pitches the book to their publishing peers and leadership. If it is accepted by the publisher for publication and the agent/author and publisher agree with the terms set forth by either party, the publisher buys the rights from the author, gives them an advance on future royalties, and assumes the fiscal responsibility for the book. Your advance may range from small sums to seven-digit figures. Traditional publishers have the resources, experience, knowledge, and established contacts to promote your book. They design, package, print, market, and distribute the book to the reading public.

This process may take a year or several years depending on when the publisher schedules your book for publication. This is why many agents include a clause in the publishing contract requiring the book to be published within 12 to 24 months or the rights revert back to the author.

Some additional cons associated with traditional publishing are:

◈ You have very little control over the title and cover design of your book.

◈ A publisher can make edits you don't agree with.

◈ You may only own the copyright unless your agent negotiates for more.

◈ You may have to do a book proposal which may require additional time and money.

◈ Editorial staff may change as a result of the publishing company's reorganization and your project could be discontinued.

◈ The tide of the industry may change and the selling potential of your book may change.

◈ Royalties can start roughly as low as .75 cents for every book the publisher sells. That's why it's good to have an agent negotiate your contract.

Self-Publishing

If an author decides to self-publish, he or she assumes all responsibility for the book from content creation to distribution. The author develops the content, proofreads the manuscript, gets it edited and provides funds for book cover design, layout, and printing of the book. The author is responsible for the marketing and distribution of the book and determining how many copies to be printed.

The self-published author may pay thousands of dollars to get the book ready for distribution. In exchange for their investment they have total control over the book project. Self-publishing allows an author to have control over the contents, design, and appearance of their book in addition to where it is marketed and distributed.

Some additional cons to be considered when self-publishing are:

◈ Bookstore distribution is limited because the majority of bookstore chains may not accept self-published books.

◈ You have to do your own public relations, marketing, and social media campaigns to get the word out about your book.

◈ Historically reviewers won't review self-published books.

Hybrid Authors and Hybrid Publishing

In addition to the self-published and traditional authors, another type of author is being developed: the hybrid author who pursues the best of both the traditional and self-publishing world and pursues publishing opportunities in both. Many traditionally published authors are re-releasing out of print books or deciding to publish books rejected by their editors. Some are simply realizing they want more control over their careers and are turning down six and seven figure advances from traditional publishers in favor of self-publishing. These authors know they have readers who will buy their book whether it's self-published or traditionally published so why give most of the profits to the publisher? It takes a business savvy author to navigate these waters but once you master AUTHORSHIP, you will be well on your way to making the decision which best suits you.

On the other hand, Hybrid publishers provide a smorgasbord of services to authors so it's very hard to place them into a specific category. Often they offer the services self-publishing authors require based on the expertise of the company. Such as distribution, e-book file preparation and upload, editing, proofreading, and interior and exterior design, etc.

Authors often retain approximately 60% of their net profits on print books and close to 80% on e-books. Some hybrid publishers are not discerning when it comes to who they will publish. A few companies require a book to be vetted and go before a review board before they will consider putting them in print. The best advice an author can follow when checking out a hybrid publisher is to make a list of the services you want provided for your book. Prior to approaching a company do your research and talk to authors who have used their services before. Hybrid publishing is fairly new, but it allows you to share the responsibility of getting your book published with a team of professionals all housed in the same company. It's called convenience and if you are as busy as most people having the help to fulfill your God calling can be a blessing.

The AUTHORSHIP Models for Self and Traditional Publishing

The genesis for this book came as I spoke with numerous authors who did not consider themselves business moguls. It was as if they were afraid they would become miniature "sharks" if they did so. I say, "What's wrong with that?" Mastering the business of writing makes you a better writer and a better businessperson.

The sharks: Barbara Corcoran, Mark Cuban, Lori Greiner, Robert Herjavec, Daymond John, and Kevin O'Leary have perfected their expertise through self-discipline and hard work making huge personal sacrifices to obtain their wealth. They have become widely known for their no nonsense natures and consistent pursuit of excellence. They raise the bar high for aspiring entrepreneurs because they know what it takes to achieve the level of success that's their trademark.

Writing a book with a business emphasis requires you strive for mastery. Even if you don't want to quit your day job and pursue a writing career, your end product (or book in this case) should be the best possible representative of you. Your book will travel to places that, perhaps, you have never been. At the very least your product is your literary calling card.

As a writer in pursuit of a successful writing career, you must change your perspective to that of a business person which must be reflected in your portfolio. At your best, you are an entrepreneur. The difference is, an entrepreneur is a creator or originator of a business idea or concept and nurtures it through the implementation stage. A businessperson on the other hand can assume a position anywhere in the business cycle wherever they have the expertise. They do not have to be the founder or originator of the idea or concept; they just need to know how to perform their job proficiently.

I realized early in this game if I wanted to make any money from writing, I had to see my career for what it is: a business. There is no way around it. Competition in the writing industry dictates you stay ahead of the pack. Developing a business perspective about the book you are writing opens the door to limitless opportunities for the modern day writer.

If you are following the route of a traditional publishing contract, your agent and publisher will handle a lot of the business aspects of your book; you become a partner in the process. Becoming familiar with the business aspects of publishing will make you a better partner and position you to make better choices, giving you the power to make valuable suggestions which support the successful completion of your book project. Understanding the process will also help you select the best agent, lawyer, and publisher for your project and make you a better negotiator during the contract stage of your publishing agreement.

However, in self-publishing; your posture as a writer changes somewhat, you are the President/CEO of your project. As we mentioned earlier, the self-published author has more control over the end result. Adopting trusted business principles ensures your Return On Investment (ROI) yields an anticipated profit. You must be able to put together an efficient team of experts who can edit, layout, design, and print your book. You must also find someone who is competent in marketing and distributing books or learn how to do this yourself. You're not just writing and waiting for them to come; you're putting your product within the reader's grasp through the implementation of a viable marketing plan developed after you researched your anticipated target market. To do these things successfully, you must become the expert through research and networking.

It is imperative you find out the answers early in the game so you will be in a better position to make an informed decision about how to best position your book for profitability. Planning is the first step toward successful book sales. Let's take a look at the elements of a start-up business plan and those for writing a new book.

Pause to study both startup procedures for business and writing. Notice the remarkable similarities. Early on in both situations you are required to do an assessment of what it is you bring to the table to accomplish your goals. You also are required to identify what makes your business and book project unique and what distinguishes you as better than your competition. Finally, you are encouraged to develop a team and establish collaborative relationships to achieve your ultimate goal which is to make money by delivering your message to the masses.

Elements of A Start-Up Business Plan

A. Analyze your existing assets and liabilities (What do you have to finance your business dream?)

B. Define your vision. (What is your expected outcome or customer's take away from your product or service?)

C. Establish your core values and principles. (What are the business ethics that will govern how you do business?)

D. Define your mission. (What is your purpose and reason for existing?)

E. Determine the need for your product or service. (What consumer need or want does your product or service fulfill in its respective industry?)

F. Determine your exceptionality. (What makes you different from your competition?)

G. Identify your target market. (Who will buy your product? Where are they located? How do you reach them?)

H. Create the optimum atmosphere for growth. (What business environment fosters goodwill for your customers?)

I. Establish product/service features and benefits. (What does your product or service look like? What is the WIIFM [What's In It for Me?] for potential customers?)

J. Establish strategic collaborations and partnerships. (Who can I partner with to better facilitate the launching of my new product or service?)

ELEMENTS OF A START-UP BOOK PROJECT

A. Determine what type of book you are writing. (Am I writing a fiction or non-fiction book?)

B. Determine what the proposed title will be. (What descriptive title or phrase best describes what I want to write about?)

C. Determine the book's premise. (What is my back-story?)

D. Determine the book's mission. (When my readers finish the last word of the last chapter, what do I want them to leave with?)

E. Determine what the reader will gain from the book they can share with others. (You want your readers to become "word-of-mouth" ambassadors.)?

F. Identify your book's exceptionality. (What makes your book unique? What is its exceptionality?)

G. Identify your target audience. (Who do I want to read my book?)

H. Determine who is your competition. (What other books are similar in nature and in the same genre?)

I. Identify your credentials as an expert on the subject matter. (What makes me the expert on this subject matter?) (Non-Fiction) (What has equipped you to be a master storyteller?) (Fiction)

J. Determine your marketing strategy. (How will I market this book to my potential target market? Where will I market this book? When will I market this book?)

K. Establish your literary team. (Where do I find an agent? Who are the best book publishers for my genre? What other support personnel do I need on my team?)

Now let's take a look at the AUTHORSHIP Models for Self and Traditional Publishing. AUTHORSHIP MODEL FOR SELF-PUBLISHING.

A. Evaluate your literary assets and liabilities.

B. Do a marketability analysis.

C. Do a personal financial assessment.

D. Create a dream sheet for this literary project.

E. Establish an advisory team of support professionals.

F. Develop a strategic plan.

G. Develop a marketing plan.

H. Develop a distribution plan.

I. Implement your plan.

J. Create an evaluation tool to monitor progress

AUTHORSHIP MODEL FOR TRADITIONAL PUBLISHING

(Remember you are partnering with a publisher and your involvement in the process will often be that of a consultant. Nevertheless, your contribution is a critical to the success of the book.)

A. Evaluate Your Literary Assets and Liabilities

B. Write the Content

C. Do a Good Proofread

D. Look for an Agent

E. Wait for the Prospective Agent's Final Decision

F. Agent Prepares Proposal and Sends Out to Potential Publishers

G. Agent Sends the Full Manuscript to the Identified Potential Publisher

H. When the Manuscript is Accepted Prepare for the Publisher's Edit

I. Prepare to Review Your Book Cover and Back Cover Copy

J. Prepare to Review Your Book Cover/Synopsis/Book Jacket

K. Prepare to Review Final Edits

L. Prepare for the Print Galley

M. Prepare for Distribution and Promotion

Summary

The elements of AUTHORSHIP are entrepreneurially centered. They permit you to establish a firm business foundation to successfully launch your writing project and set the stage for future ministry efforts and profitable endeavors.

If the information in this chapter seems overwhelming, don't be discouraged. Remember God has left us a model in The Nehemiah Principle to follow for the business side of writing. In the following chapters we will break it down into digestible bite size pieces.

CHAPTER FOUR

CALLED BY GOD...

ಬಂಡ

The story of Nehemiah begins much like others in the Old Testament - a regular man hearing the call of God and choosing to act on it. Nehemiah hears from a brother the conditions in Jerusalem are terrible. He was told that *"The exile survivors who are left there in the province are in bad shape. Conditions are appalling. The wall of Jerusalem is still rubble; the city gates are still cinders"* (Nehemiah 1:3). Some people would have simply chosen to ignore this call, but Nehemiah knew better. His first instinct after weeping was to spend days mourning, *"fasting and praying before the God-of-Heaven"* (Nehemiah 1:4).

Before you begin your book project, you must spend time discovering what God has in His plan for this project. Use the prayer at the end of the chapter to help you start your prayer journey. The remainder of this chapter is dedicated to helping you figure out exactly how to begin your book project.

TO WRITE OR NOT TO WRITE…
ACTING ON GOD'S CALL

If God called you to write, then your obedience to that call is required. Ask yourself why should you be a writer? Do you possess the skills to do so? If not, are you willing to get the training necessary? If you are obedient to God's call, are you looking to write a book and have it be an instant success? Think again! Writing is one of the few things you do that is frequently subjective to the opinions of others, even in Christendom. Writing well does not guarantee you best seller status. Matter of fact, there are some best sellers out there not written well but marketed well, and their authors still got the privilege of that title.

As a self-published author, you may make a sizeable investment and not reap an ROI (return on investment). As a traditionally published author, you are one of several authors represented by that agent or publisher and you may have to assist with marketing your book to get the results you desire. That's why writing as a hobby just won't do. You have to be willing to get into the PIT (putting-in-time) to see your dream realized and it may cost you some money in the process. Sometimes, it's very hard to monetize your book project. My co-authors and I spent $10,000 on our first self-published book, *Songs of Three Sisters,* a Christian poetry book based on the poetry and wisdom books of the bible and we have given away more books than we sold.

So, you may ask if you feel like you're not a good writer or writing is too hard; and you may not make any money, then why bother?

Those are good valid questions and ones you should answer fairly early in the game. The celebrity status associated with being a writer is seductive. People instantly offer you respect when they find out you crafted a book. You are immediately labeled an "expert" and invited to the front of the room. Even when you tell people you are writing a book they become star struck. As a result, you wear the crown until some noted literary expert actually does a critique of your not-so-well-written book. Readers are fickle and writers are even more so, thus, your popularity can change overnight, bringing with it the discouragement which has signaled an early end to the career of so many emerging writers. Right now is the time for you to do an honest assessment of your intent to become an author. That is the purpose of this chapter, to seal the deal by helping you to answer the question: **to write or not to write?** Frankly if you are writing for personal gain, then it's a profession or career not a calling. You are called to write when:

- ❖ You will do it for free.
- ❖ People tell you their lives were changed as a result of something you wrote.
- ❖ You don't do it to stroke your ego or build your self-importance, you do it to glorify God and help others.
- ❖ You want to master it.
- ❖ It's not a means to an end but an end in itself.
- ❖ God told you He called you to do so.
- ❖ There is confirmation of your gift from experts in your industry.

Now, let's talk about why you should be a writer. You should be a writer if you must write. If God gave you a yearning to write that you can't run from, then you must write. It's like breathing, you have to do it or die. Maya Angelou says, "There is no greater agony than bearing an untold story inside you." I equate my need to write with my child birthing experience. It was painful but it was worth it. To be one with my Creator in the birthing process was one of the greatest gifts I've ever received. Writing has the capacity to bring you great joy. Sometimes you have to wait for that joy, but if you write a good book, it will come. When someone calls and tells you they were stuck in the middle of a book project and their only salvation was your book that's something to shout about. Or when someone that was contemplating ending it all picks up your book and decides life is worth living after reading it, surely that's worth the blood, sweat, and tears you invested. These things have happened to me as an author and I am humbled to say the God inspired words I have written have changed the lives of others.

Writing allows you to leave a literary legacy that cannot be erased. The bible is a prime example of a living work which continues to speak to the hearts of its readers and changes their lives for an eternity. That power is invested in you as a writer. Use it wisely and you can change worlds and shape nations.

As a writer, you get to become a tour guide. The dictates of your mind can create new adventures for your readers. They can travel to foreign lands, another state, city or even to outer space without leaving the comfort of their homes as a result of your efforts. You can put them in a time machine and take them to another time, place, and another experience. As a writer, you've got power!

One of my favorite classes in high school was Literature. The Odyssey and Iliad by Homer sparked my love for reading books other than Harlequin romance novels because of their thought provoking poetry. I was stretched beyond my cultural experience and gained an appreciation for the beauty of prose.

Now, let's look at some ways you can strengthen your writing skill level.

Look for examples of good writing from best-selling authors and analyze them. Interview editors of the magazines, newspapers, or journals you read and ask them what they consider to be good writing.

Look for The Six Traits of Good Writing: the ideas and content (is it interesting), the organization, the voice, word choice, sentence fluency and the grammar. Let's take a look at the definitions of The Six Traits of Good Writing:

What Are the Six Traits?*

Ideas - Good writing has clear ideas, a purpose, or focus. It should have specific ideas and details.

Organization - Writing should have a beginning, middle, and an ending and be well organized and easy to follow.

Voice - Your writing should connect with your audience, fit your purpose for writing, and reveal your voice.

Word Choice - Good writing has specific nouns, verbs, and strong words which deliver the writer's message.

Sentence Fluency - Sentences should vary in length, with a variety of sentence beginnings. The writing should flow smoothly from sentence to sentence.

Conventions - Strong writing is edited for grammar, punctuation, capitalization, and spelling so the writer's ideas are easily understood.

*Taken From Great Source *Iwrite*

Here's a list of things you can do to develop your writing skills for mastery.

Practical Tips for New Writers

⬦ Keep a notebook about your observations and those of your resources and reference them when writing your next novel or book. Make notes of what works and what doesn't work so you can avoid the pitfall of a bad writing habit.

⬦ Read good writing based on your research, so you can identify it when you write it. Reading can also help you improve your spelling, sentence structure, punctuation, and vocabulary.

◈ Take writing courses and seminars to improve your weaknesses and to maintain your strengths as a writer. Keep a journal of the nuggets you learn in these classes and incorporate them into your writing plan for improving your skill.

◈ Build a writing library containing tools such as the Chicago Manual of Style or the MLA Book of Style, and Webster's New World Dictionary so you have them at your fingertips when you need them.

◈ Set aside some time on a regular basis to practice your craft the way athletes and musicians do. They become the "best" by going above and beyond the expectations of others to learn and practice their craft until those skills become second nature to them. So learn, learn, learn and write, write, write.

◈ Become a part of a local writer's critique group and get the feedback and nurturing you need to become a better writer. Go to Meetup.com or Google, "local writers group," to locate them in your area.

◈ Find opportunities to write and seek reviews from experts. LinkedIn has several writer's groups and I see postings by reviewers quite regularly soliciting the opportunity to review your work. Remember, the critic can be your best friend. There's nothing like constructive criticism when you are in the perfecting mode and perfection is a lifelong process.

◈ Seek the advice of experts and make the necessary modifications in your writing. A good copy editor looks for patterns of strengths and weaknesses in your writing.

I had an editor text me about a book I wrote; she loved the book and shared with me some minor changes I could do to make it better. I was thrilled to get her insight and it was free.

You may find though you have the passion for writing, you lack the skill. Don't let this discourage you. Having weak areas in your writing ability does not disqualify you as a writer. In fact, being honest about your deficiencies and making the necessary adjustments actually makes you a better writer.

Both entrepreneurship and AUTHORSHIP require you to take a risk, a calculated one if you follow the advice given in this book. Entrepreneurs frequently don't see a profit in their business in the first three years of operation. Are they bad at business as a result? No. Likewise, your first book may not see immediate success either. There are challenges you will face on your way to becoming a good writer with a marketable product if perfecting your craft is one of them, you are in great company. All authors should be striving to be better at what they do If you accept this challenge you are already one step ahead in the writing game.

Now that you've answered the "to write or not write" question, it's time to move on to establishing some type of plan practical foundational elements to give you a better snapshot of where you are headed in regard to product creation. Happy Writing!

Developing a Plan Fit for the Master's Use

Trust in the LORD with all your heart and lean not on your own understanding; in all your ways submit to him, and he will make your paths straight. **Proverbs 3:5-6**

Nehemiah was a man who knew how to plan. He sought God about the problem and developed a plan with the help of the Holy Spirit to remedy the situation. He was successful because he humbled himself before God, recognizing he could do nothing without His intervention. Seeking God for guidance is like taking a test in school and having all the answers on the test paper, you may have to search for them but they are there. Seek God for divine direction. Ask Him for the wisdom and favor you need to start your book project and you to, will be able to create a plan for the Master's use.

GETTING STARTED

Perhaps, you have some writing skills, but don't know where to start. Once I decided to become serious about my craft, I started taking workshops, going to writer's conventions, and dialoguing with other writers to determine the best starting point for me. They suggested I follow this pathway:

❖ *Write about what you know (and make sure you know it really well):* A wise older friend gave me some invaluable advice, "Find a problem and become an expert on the solution." Your years of experience and education may have equipped you to address these areas of concern in your industry. Put it in writing and share it with your peers.

◈ *Start off small*: Try writing an article for a local newspaper or magazine and gauge the reaction to your contribution or identify what periodicals are associated with your profession and become a contributing writer for them.

◈ Internet writing is also a great place to start. There are numerous e-magazines constantly looking for articles from great writers. They provide the opportunity to be published and the benefit of having an editor on board to take your article from good to great.

◈ *It's time to go to the next level,* **Blogging***!*: What is a blog? A blog is an on-line journal or diary. What is a blogger? A blogger is someone who blogs or writes content for a blog. You can actually be a guest on a blog. How regularly should you blog? A blog is updated frequently. If scheduled, it takes a small portion of your day to complete. I know bloggers who sit down and write all of their blogs for a week and post as needed. Talk about instant feedback on your writing, other people can also comment or respond to your blog post.

◈ *Now you've mastered the small stuff ...*: Writing your first book can be intimidating, but if you have practiced and perfected your writing skills, you are more than ready for the big time. If you decided to blog, you could take your blogs and use them to build content for a book or you could start from scratch if you like, but whatever you do realize it's going to require lots of time management and dedication to project completion.

If timidity has you in neutral, partnering with a seasoned writer or writers by participating in a compilation may be a great place for you to start. This is where you contribute a chapter to a book that is a variation of an agreed upon theme. I did this in *Ready, Set, Succeed, Making Your Dreams Come True*. I partnered with eight other authors to write a book about success. I am a master networker and I met a young man at a speaker's competition who introduced me to this opportunity. My first self-published book, *Songs of Three Sisters*, was co-authored with two other poets. We took our literary works and categorized them based on the poetry and wisdom books of the bible and included our personal testimonies.

Today, you have the advantage of e-book publishing which allows you the luxury of writing a book and test driving it on a major publisher's site such as Amazon. It's cost effective and it allows you to have a genuine AUTHORSHIP experience. Take a lesson learned approach and when you are ready to really step out there and "get it done," you will be more prepared to do so because you practiced, practiced, and practiced. The results being that you are not only a better writer, but you are also a better authorpreneur for the glory of God's kingdom.

The most comfortable position a writer can assume is writing about something they know about. Don't compromise your vision and sell out to writing about what's popular in the industry at that time. Wait for your season, it will come. Ecclesiastes 3:1 states, "That there is an appointed time for everything." There is plenty to do in the interim to perfect your craft. Take advantage of the writer's groups, conferences, and books available to help you do that.

Passion also plays an important role in choosing the topic you want to write about. That's why it is important to write the passion of your heart. Authors are my passion. Years ago I fell in love with those who were able to provide me with a pleasurable escape. I have spent the last decade sowing into their lives by entertaining, empowering, and equipping them to tell their stories. It is my hope and prayer whatever your topic and however you choose to share it, the reward will far exceed your expectation and be a blessing to the readers who explore its pages. Happy Writing!

"Fill your paper with the breathings of your heart." ~William Wordsworth

Go ye and Plan ...

"For I know the plans I have for you," says the Lord. "They are plans for good and not for disaster, to give you a future and a hope." Jeremiah 29:11 (NLT)

Jeremiah 29:11 is one of my life scriptures. I rest easier at night knowing God is the Master Publisher in my life. Acknowledging that does not prohibit me from developing a plan. On the contrary, it actually enhances my responsibility to do so as a steward of all I have been given by Him in order to have a "future and a hope."

My dear sisters and brothers of the pen, stuff happens and you will need something to get you back on track when it does. Your plan will do just that. A plan also solidifies your intent to complete a thing. If it's in writing on paper and you have expelled the energy to put it there, most likely you won't rest until it's done.

Your plan is a roadmap to get you to your destination, an anchor when all else is bound up in chaos. A dream on the other hand keeps you above it all. It is the fuel that starts your implementation sequence. It's the positive motivation to keep you on course and the satisfaction you get when you cross the finish line, which in our case, is the last word spoken or written before "The End."

So let's get busy, prepping for the journey!

CHAPTER FIVE

PREPAIRING FOR THE JOURNEY

ℰᏰ

PURSUING THE DREAM

We all have dreams, spoken and unspoken, genuine or fantasy. There are times in our lives when we wish and hope for things that are beyond our present reach which often require supernatural intervention. A dream is more than a midnight reverie. It is something embedded in your core and you can't run away from it because it's with you always. It has the propensity to outlive you and be carried on the shoulders of your children.

As a writer, I have a dream. My dream is to write a fiction novel. I have been addicted to romance novels since my tween years. I've danced on the outskirts of this dream because I am in awe of the way master novelists craft a story that will keep you coming back for more.

I recently met one of my favorite romance writers, Deanne Gist. I got to interview her during the Romantic Times Booklovers Convention in Kansas City. I was thrilled. Historical Romance is one of my absolute favorites and she has mastered the art of storytelling in that genre. My gift as an advocate for writers has been the opportunity to get to know and interview some of the greatest in the industry, but I am always awestruck by my favorites. I immediately become a groupie. I start sweating profusely, getting tongue tied, and I always do something terribly embarrassing. So, how am I going to get the advice I need in order to get started? Push fear out of the way and realize my dream.

Fear only meets its match when it comes face-to-face with the truth. How are you handling your FEAR (False Evidence Appearing Real) of pursuing your dream? There are four things you can do in order to birth your book baby:

1. *Accept the fact you are a writer.* Own it and wear it proudly. It is your truth, to deny it is akin to denying your existence.

2. *Kick out those negative spies in your land that keep stealing your fruit.* You have the power to possess the land just like Joshua and the children of Israel, shout down the Jericho Wall's in your life which prohibit you from possessing your dream.

3. *Your dream may be a puzzle that just needs to be put together.* Adopt a Nike attitude and "Just Do It!", but don't do that

until you are well versed in how to pursue it by doing the necessary research to find the right pathway for you.

4. *Get help.* You don't have to go it alone. There is safety in a multitude of counselors.

Don't believe the dream stealers when they tell you the following about pursuing your dreams:

5. *It's impossible.* It's only impossible if you don't attempt to do anything about the pursuit of your dream.

6. *Don't quit your day job. You don't have the right stuff to be a writer.* There are numerous resources out there to assist in equipping you to write a novel or non-fiction book. We all have an imagination and are experts in something. If it's your passion, pursue it.

7. *The market is so saturated.* There is always room in the industry for good writers.

8. *Anybody can write a book.* Yes, that is true, but can they write a readable, marketable book that has the potential to climb the best seller list?

9. *You don't need any help. They're just telling you that because they want your money.* A football team goes a lot further when the entire team is trying to win the game versus a single player. Making a plan to win and acquiring the necessary resources to win at the writing game is critical to your success. Once you have a budget in place for your book project that will be your guide in determining how much money to spend on those resources.

10. *Where are you going to find the time to do that?* You make time for the things you have a passion for; if writing is your passion, it will become a priority.

11. *That's nice, but you need to be more responsible than that.* In Ecclesiastes, Solomon says that there is a season for everything. If you have determined that now is your season for writing your book, then the most responsible thing to do is to "JUST DO IT!"

12. *Where are you going to get the money?* Money is not necessary to get started, but a plan and a budget is critical. Once you've evaluated your financial status, determine where and when you can start working on your writing goals based on your existing resources.

Real Talk for Writers Who Want to Make Money Selling Books

In this country, you can have just about anything you want, if you are willing to work for it. So, yes, my bright-eyed optimistic friend, you can be a best-selling author. If you don't mind a little delayed gratification and are willing to make a few sacrifices, you can be one of the millions of people in America who are making money while they sleep. "How?" You may ask. Well, you can do this by making a plan and developing a strategy which pays dividends, but doesn't pull you away from your main source of income.

Rarely have I met an author or aspiring author, who did not have best seller "stars" in their eyes. Birthing a book is similar to birthing a baby. Most parents want the best for their children especially first-time parents who are mesmerized by their little creation. First time authors feel the same about their initial publication. Their literary "baby" can do no wrong and they dare the experts to say otherwise. Eventually, the "first timers" come to the ultimate conclusion creating a book that tops the bestseller lists is a rarity the first time out of the gate.

It's okay to have a bestseller dream, but you must respect the process. It will require a commitment to seeing this thing through to completion and consistency in implementing your plan. The end product in this case, a book is the true measure of your parenting skills. As a writer the reception of your literary baby by potential readers and industry experts after its completion, dictates your sales. These are the indicators you've done a great job or a not so great job with your book.

WWW.Dictionary.com defines "bestseller" as: "a book that is among those having the largest sales during a given period." People sometimes write books because they want to make money, and lots of it. Potential writers are regularly courted with glossy high cost ads from dubious solicitors that promise them the world with titles that proclaim, "You Can Become a Best-Selling Author in 90 Days!" or "How to Sell 10,000 books in One Week!" Beware!

Bestsellers are determined by their rankings in sales in comparison to other books in that genre for a particular time period. There is no magic number qualifying you for that status. For example, if the book *Heaven is for Real* sold 25,000 copies the first week of

January and Diary of a Wimpy Kid (Cabin Fever) sold 25,001, it would be the best-selling book for the week.

The USA Today's Best Selling Books List is determined by how many of your books are reported as sold by the top booksellers in the U.S. during that week. As you can see, the main objective is to sell books and lots of them. Your book can achieve bestseller status, but it takes time and book sales to make it happen. Anything is possible considering there are 52 weeks in a year and you only have to make it during one of those weeks to wear the title of best-selling author, which means you can go out and buy the t-shirt.

Most business owners don't start out anticipating they will fail in their business endeavor. They proceed with confidence because they believe in their mission and its salability. That first guy who had the idea of moving beyond the industry paradigm of printing a book to making it available in an electronic format and selling it to his customers was an innovator. Now, thousands of people are following his lead and telling their story in an e-book format. Writing a book is a business venture. The author should expect to succeed if the product entertains, educates, informs, or inspires. In the case of ministry, expect to succeed if it changes lives, renews minds, and brings revelation. For those of you who are ministry minded this next section is for you.

Write The Vision and Make It Plain

When I was teaching business classes, my students from middle school to college loved creating a dream board. They brought in poster board and I supplied the magazines, newspapers, glue sticks, and markers. I gave them a topic and they used their imaginations to create their dream boards. Your assignment is to create a dream board which depicts your writing dream in live and living color. Have fun and share it with your advisory team.

If you are not an artsy crafty kind of person perhaps making a dream list would suffice for you. Develop a list of all the things you want to achieve as a writer this year, both personal and professional goals. Put them in outline format based on priority and assign a date for completion. Once you've done that review each goal and develop a step-by-step procedure you plan on using to implement each of those goals. I use sticky notes to post my goals and then I place them on an empty wall in my bedroom.. As a result, I am reminded of them every day when I get up and when lay down each night. Some people prefer using 3x5 cards to write down their goals. Review them at least twice a day or perhaps imagine how it will feel to accomplish them and add any new inspired action steps to your plan. Don't wait to celebrate once you've accomplished all of your goals. Do something nice for yourself at the completion of each major goal along the way. Make sure you add your goals to a calendar or develop a timeline (dividing your goals into daily, weekly, monthly, yearly increments) so you can modify and adjust your goals when necessary. Remember you have developed an overall plan to realize your goals. Stick with it and you will ultimately see the manifestation of your dream.

As I mentioned in the introduction, discovering your gift is more than an intellectual acknowledgment. It must become a part of your soul. Once the gift is established in your subconscious your actions will follow. It should reflect your desire to deliver a quality product to your readers.

Your job description as a writer is to "communicate information and inspire people to act."[1] It doesn't matter what the genre is. If you are not convinced you are a writer and the evidence is not reflected in your product, you might as well say writing is your hobby. You do it solely to entertain yourself. Most people who are writers either have a story to tell or want to share their intellectual capital with the world. Having writing as a hobby is nice, but it doesn't put money in your bank account or get your message to the masses; mastering the art of AUTHORSHIP will.

Once you decide to become serious about your craft, the universe reaches out to greet you. It's not some mystical magical thing you can turn on or off at will. It's a universal law that you become more of what you think about. Proverbs 23:7 supports this law: "*As a man thinketh* in his heart, *so is he*." When it comes to writing, you should never ask yourself the Shakespearean question, "To be, or not to be," which was good writing by the way. Like Shakespeare, you should be convinced of your writing ability and aspire to be the best writer there ever was.

Your next consideration should be the reader, your anticipated target audience. You write so others can read your work. When writing, you want to invoke the five senses: hearing, sight, touch, smell and taste. To do it, you must step out of your comfort zone as the writer and put yourself in the place of the reader. Readers buy books to be informed, entertained, or because it's required reading in a college English class. If you successfully satisfy the reader's yearning for a good read, he or she will be back for more; standing in line before the bookstore opens waiting for your next novel. Determine early in the game to respect your readers. They deserve to be seriously considered when developing your plan of action.

In the early part of my writing journey, my passion to write was fuel enough to push me to take the risk of exposing my written thoughts to the world. Since then, my readers have caused me to want to be the best writer possible simply because I hold a keen appreciation for their loyalty and I respect them. You must do the same when you are developing your subject matter. Show the reader respect by delivering a quality product that is correct, entertaining, and memorable. Your attitude in the pursuit of your excellence as a writer is evidence of your conviction to do so. So yes, sometimes it is all about you!

EVALUATE YOUR LITERARY ASSETS AND LIABILITIES

When you publish a book, you are selling your readers on more than the opportunity to read a great book, you are selling them you! Too often authors get so caught up in delivering the message in the book they forget to prepare themselves for their contribution to the creditability of their project. With millions of books in bookstores, online and across the country, screaming "Buy Me!" you have to do something or possess something which makes your product different or unique. Talent is a great thing to have, and you are now on a mission to let the world have the pleasure of enjoying "you," and that talent. You can be an asset to the marketing and delivery of your message by utilizing your talents to promote your book. Now's the time to do an evaluation of what you personally bring to the table in the form of education, experience, and exceptionality, the three "E's" that will benefit your reader.

EDUCATION

◈ Go dig up those old transcripts to identify if your academic pursuits lend credibility to your book's subject matter. What courses have you taken that introduced you to your topic?

◈ What internships or student teaching and volunteer assignments prepared you to be an expert on this subject matter?

◈ What were the credentials of the professors who taught you the subject matter? If there is a fit, could they be prime candidates to endorse your book?

◈ Is your Alma Mater highly revered in the literary industry for producing experts on your topic?

EXPERIENCE

Pull out your most current resume, curriculum vitae, speaker's one sheet, or press kit and scan it to identify all of your professional pursuits which support your expertise on the topics discussed in your book.

◇ What professional or personal experiences validate your creditability as an expert on this topic?

◇ What professional associations or organizations authenticate your capability to perform a certain task related to your topic?

◇ Who has previously endorsed you or your expertise?

◇ What professional or personal experiences have enabled you to give an intellectual or experiential discourse on your subject matter? (For example have you done speeches, workshops, been on a panel, webinars or tele-classes on your topics.)

◇ What professional experiences have you had that allow you to give an experiential recollection on your subject matter?

◇ What quantitative and qualitative statements on your resume or curriculum vitae support your expertise on your particular topic?

◇ What professional people have you networked or worked with that can act as a support system in the areas you don't quite have the expertise in regarding your topic?

◇ What professionals in your industry do you have access to who are authorities on your subject matter?

EXCEPTIONALITY

We all have things in our lives which make us unique. Do a personal inventory and list those things making you "special." Some factors to consider while doing so:

◈ What life experiences have you had that support your ability to discuss your topic adequately?

◈ What qualities do you possess that contribute to your capability to discuss this subject matter proficiently?

◈ What aspects of your ancestry contribute to you having a particular exceptionality?

◈ What unusual event or events have shaped your knowledge or perception of your subject matter?

◈ What historical episode or occurrence inspired you to research your topic?

◈ What tragedy or dramatic life changing event empowered you to write about your topic?

Now that you've gotten a better snapshot of your assets, let's take a moment to look at your liabilities. Ask yourself the following questions:

◈ Are you a beginning writer or seasoned writer? Take a close look at the current industry to better be able to define what characteristics are associated with being a beginning writer or a seasoned writer.

◈ If you are a beginning writer who has chosen self-publishing, do you have a good editor? Ask for referrals from authors in your network. Develop a questionnaire and interview potential candidates.

❖ If you are going the traditional publishing route, do you have an agent? If not, do you know how to find one? Do you know how to write a query letter?

❖ Have you put together your support team? Talk with seasoned writers to get referrals. This is not the place to take short cuts. Assembling a strong support team of professionals who can help you with your book is essential. Don't compromise your message by turning out a shabby product. (Remember your book is your business card. It is a reflection of your expertise.)

❖ If you are a seasoned writer, have you done your professional success? Are you living the dream? Have you accomplished your goals and objectives for establishing a writing career?

❖ Are you current on social media? Do you have a Facebook, Pinterest, LinkedIn, Instagram, Twitter account?

❖ Do you network? Do you attend writer's conferences or belong to a writers group? Have you joined writer's groups on Meetup.com in your area?

❖ Do you enter writer's contests? (A great way to get some FREE PR. Also, a great opportunity to raise money for your book project if you are self-publishing.)

❖ Have you taken advantage of the benefits being associated with book clubs bring to authors?

❖ Have you done a blog book tour?

❖ Are the marketing materials for your book effective tools to help you reach your target audience?

Here are some suggestions for doing a literary analysis:

◈ Host a focus group with your target market and ask them the hard questions about your last product. Is the title memorable? Is your book cover alluring? What is the mission of the book? Would they pay the asking price for a book of this nature? Would they recommend it to a friend? How would they make it better? What would they change? Would they like to see it as an e-book? Are the graphics suitable for the topic?

◈ Do a Literary SWOT Analysis on your last book project. The SWOT analysis is a strategic analysis which deals with the strengths, weaknesses, opportunities, and threats associated with a project. Your prior knowledge of the industry will assist you in making a proper assessment of:

◈ The strengths of the project

  A. What are readers saying they love about your book?

  B. What has your agent said is the marketing point of difference for your book? (In other words, what are the areas in which your book is completely different in a way the market wants and values.)

  C. Why did your publisher pick your book over hundreds of others? What was your unique sales proposition, the factor or consideration you presented as the reason your book is different from and better than others of the same subject or genre?

◈ The weaknesses of that the project

    A. What are readers saying they don't like about the book?

    B. What are reviewers saying they don't like about the book?

    C. Did you reach your expected goal for the sales of the book? If not evaluate why not.

◈ The opportunities associated with this project

    A. Did this book introduce you to new markets?

    B. Has it increased your credibility as an author in the marketplace?

    C. Has this book increased the sales on your other books?

◈ The threats to this project

    A. Is the market flooded with books of this type in your genre?

    B. Are you a new author?

    C. If self-published, do you have the funds to successfully complete this project?

    D. If traditionally published will you sell enough books to earn out your advance?

    E. How much marketing will the publishing house actually do and how much of the burden will fall on you?

Summary

Use the information gathered from these two activities to assist you in making better business decisions in the future. Even the best authors may need a Christian AUTHORSHIP tune-up! In the next chapter, we will take a look at actually developing a plan. Until then, Happy Writing!

CHAPTER SIX

DEVELOPING A PLAN
FIT FOR THE MASTER

හිටෙ

After Nehemiah spent days of fasting and prayer, he felt confident in what God was calling him to do. He decided the best way to help Jerusalem was to rebuild it, so he asked the king's blessing to lead the rebuilding project. *"If it please the king, and if the king thinks well of me, send me to Judah, to the city where my family is buried, so that I can rebuild it."* (Nehemiah 2:5). The key thing to remember here is that Nehemiah's plan is fully developed *before* coming to the king, keeping in mind he'd already figured out what tools he will need, how long it would take, and how many helper's he would need. *"The king, with the queen sitting alongside him, said, "How long will your work take and when would you expect to return?" I gave him a time, and the king gave his approval to send me. Then I said, "If it please the king, provide me with letters to the governors across the Euphrates that authorize my travel through to Judah; and also an order to Asaph, keeper of the king's forest, to supply me with timber for the beams of The Temple fortress, the wall of the city, and the house where I'll be living."* (Nehemiah 2:6-8).

Before beginning your book project, you need to follow Nehemiah's example and create a plan not just for writing the book, but for marketing and selling your book. This chapter will give you a strategy to help you develop your plan.

STRATEGICALLY SPEAKING

Developing a Strategic Plan

"Hello, my name is Sharon and I am directionally challenged."

I was thrilled when they first came out with MapQuest. Ordinarily I would drive around the city lost for hours sometimes not getting to my destination at all, the innovation of MapQuest was a dream come true. Then they invented the GPS and I'd thought I died and went to heaven. Until I accidentally slammed my GPS connector in my car door one day. I watched horrified as it crumbled into a million little pieces. A mishap which could have been easily avoided if I had not been rushing at 100 mph to get somewhere I thought was important. I live in the 4th largest city in America and my GPS is—or was until its untimely demise—one of my closest friends. The pain of losing my intimate companion, who I relied on to take me to places unknown, started memories of

The Twilight Zone episodes flooding through my brain. Perhaps I was in an alternate universe dreaming of this awful event and when I was fortunate enough to wake up from my dream, all would be well. Or would it? The first stage of grief had started. I was deadlocked in denial. I went on to further reminisce of the movie, *Groundhog Day*, and prayed my fate would not be that of Bill Murray where I relived this adventure, over and over again without resolution. Thank God reality eventually slapped me in the face and the memory of my dearly departed friend made me run to my computer and seek an economical replacement. I rely heavily on my GPS much like you will come to depend on your well-thought out strategic plan for the delivery of a successful book project. Let's take a look at a popular business tool, the strategic plan.

What is a strategy?

A strategy is a plan, approach, or line of attack to accomplish a specific goal or objective.

What is a strategic plan?

A strategic plan is a well thought out researched course of action to accomplish something.

Why is it important for an author to develop a strategic plan?

A strategic plan provides a comprehensive roadmap for the author's completed book project. It assists in evaluating the integrity of the book idea, allows an opportunity to streamline the processes, and facilitates the development of a realistic timeline for project completion.

Before you begin the process of developing a strategic plan for your book project, let's do a review. We've discussed some of these questions in previous chapters, now you get an opportunity to put some of that knowledge to work. (It's like being prepared for an exam in school, if you've done the hard work prior to this, you already have the answers.) In order to develop a concrete plan of action which may determine the future of your project, ask yourself the following questions:

◈ Are you SOLD on your book idea? Is God calling you to write this book?

◈ What is your "why" for this book project?

◈ Is your buy-in to this idea strong enough to withstand the hurdles which accompany seeing this project to the end?

◈ Will you defend your premise before your most formidable foe?

◈ What makes you an expert on the subject matter you will discuss in your book?

◈ What education or experience have you had that supports your expertise to discuss this subject?

◈ Is there enough information on your topic available to warrant writing a book?

◈ If you are not an expert, is there adequate research or resources available for you to comprehensively cover this topic?

◈ Is your subject matter broad enough?

◈ Is your subject matter extensive enough to appeal to the general populace or a larger target market?

What does your competition look like? A trip to the library to look at the Book of Lists can help you determine what books are out there which cover your topic. Also a visit to your local bookstore, or www.barnesandnoble.com or www.Amazon.com can assist you in identifying current book releases on your topic.

Is your subject matter a carbon copy of another author's work?

◈ Research the historical sales data of books like yours that have had success in your genre for new authors. For example, if you are looking for current sales figures, you can use Amazon.com to get a general idea. Nielsen BookScan is also a source for point-of-sale data.

◈ Who wants to read your book?

◈ Is there a large enough niche of potential readers to support your investment of time, money, and intellectual capital? I've known several authors who wrote books out of their passion. Unfortunately, it takes more than passion about your topic to sell books. I would recommend you do an electronic survey, (creating one on www.surveymonkey. com, it's free) and query a sample group of potential readers who may be interested in your topic. You can also get a report of their responses and include your findings in your strategic plan, or host a focus group to examine the feasibility of your book idea.

◈ Is your topic brandable and bankable?

◈ What unique marketing approach can you develop to make your book unforgettable?

◈ Is your book timely? Are you writing about a topic which has relevance for an audience "for such a time as this?"

◈ Research the longevity of similar books and query new writers in your genre to make an informed decision about your book's potential in today's market.

◈ Does your book idea have spinoff potential or the ability to become a series?

◈ Brainstorm like titles for topics covered in your book which would make great companions to your existing idea. If it works, you have spinoff or series potential. Incorporate this into your strategic plan.

◈ Does your book have national and international charisma?

◈ Think book sales! Is it relevant to a national audience? Can you sell your book around the world? Is the subject matter relevant to someone in Ireland or Ghana?

◈ Are you self-publishing your book or seeking a contract with a conventional publishing house?

◈ In Self-publishing the writer is responsible for the production, marketing, and distribution of the book. A traditional publisher contracts for the rights to publish an author's book and does the production, marketing, and distribution of the book at the publisher's expense. They pay the author a percentage or royalties based on the number of books sold. There are numerous resources to help you make this decision, available on-line, at your local bookstores and libraries.

◈ Don't forget to make room for your passion in this process, loving what you do helps to make even the most arduous task enjoyable and it's a critical component for making it to the finish line.

Now that you've examined your book idea thoroughly, let's look at developing a sustaining strategy to help you move forward.

As a business person, I've seen strategic plans the size of dissertations. That's not our goal or objective here. Our objective is to implement the KISS (Keep It Simple Sweetie) Principle. I want you to have something you can glance at on a daily basis that will encourage and empower you. So I am introducing two pictographic forms of media you can use to capture your strategic plan on one page. Let your creative juices flow and enjoy the process. This is the place where you get to take all of that passion and put it to work. So let's get busy!

Create a Vision Board or an Infographic

Earlier we talked about creating a dream board. A vision board is very similar except on a dream board you might put things that are out of your present reach. Whereas on a vision board you will actually put tangible goals you can achieve. You would list your goals, find pictures which adequately represent them in magazines, newspapers, stock photos, etc. Include motivational scriptures that encourage and exhort you to stay focused. Don't forget to place the dream board where you can see it daily. Evaluate it on a quarterly basis to see if you need to change anything and when you reach your goals, don't forget to throw a celebration.

Another tool you can use when developing your plan is an infographic or information graphics. Wikipedia defines an Information graphics, or infographics as "graphic visual representations of information, data or knowledge intended to present complex information quickly and clearly. They can improve cognition by utilizing graphics to enhance the human visual system's ability to see patterns and trends. The process of creating infographics can be referred to as data visualization, information design, or information architecture." www.slideshare. net is an excellent tool for creating infographics and there are several presentations on infographics about, guess what, "infographics." Actually, Slide Share is an excellent resource for writers. There is an infographic on Slide Share titled, *Why Infographics Are Important*, check it out.

Also Slide Share (http://www.slideshare.net) is a great place to do research on how to do almost anything. If you want a more extensive list of instructions on how to create a dream board or infographics, go to Slide Share. The next best DIY base for instruction is YouTube. If you are a visual learner, it's a great place to see how to accomplish almost any task.

Summary

Developing a strategic plan for your book should be one of the initial things you do as a writer. For a traditional writer, it helps you deliver a good product to your publisher and acts a roadmap for your writing career. For the self-published author, it forces you to ask the hard questions about your intellectual and financial investment. Is my subject matter pertinent in today's society? Am I geographically available for international distribution? Is there a market for my expertise? How can I access it? How much should I charge for my book? What will the market support? These are all questions you as an author will eventually ask yourself. Your strategic plan will act as a literary GPS to assist you in intentionally getting to your destination. Remember to dream big and work your strategic plan!

In *Christian AUTHORSHIP, Mastering the Business of Publishing*, Rochelle Carter will actually discuss in detail how to do a Book Business Plan. Make sure you go out and get your copy today!

Note: Go to my Pinterest account at https://www.pinterest. com/sharoncjenkins/for examples of a vision/dream board and infographic for the traditional and self-published author on the *Christian AUTHORSHIP* tab.

CHAPTER SEVEN

NOW IT'S TIME TO BUILD YOUR MANUSCRIPT

ಶ丿ೕ

*S*o *we built the wall and the whole wall was joined together to half its height, for the people had a mind to work.* **Nehemiah 4:6**

Do you have a mind to work? Nehemiah's passion to rebuild Jerusalem was infectious. The people were so motivated by the task at hand even their enemies could not stop them from accomplishing their goal to complete the wall. If you have a mind to work than nothing can stop you from completing the task of writing your manuscript.

A manuscript is a draft or a book in the development stage. It's an author's attempt to clearly communicate their message in written form for the education, entertainment, or exhortation of their reading audience. Typically, a fiction novel runs around 80,000 to 110,000 words and a nonfiction book runs between 25,000 to

100,000 words. The average publisher requests your book be at least 70,000 words or more. To determine how long your book will be in its finished state, divide the number of words you have by 250 and you will come up with an estimated final page count.

Your content usually dictates your chapter length and the number of chapters in the book. The best way to determine chapter size is to research your preferences as a reader. Browse through some of your favorite books in your genre and use your preferences as a guide.

Your book is usually divided into three sections:

Front Matter

- ◈ Title Page
- ◈ Copyright Page
- ◈ Dedication
- ◈ Acknowledgements
- ◈ Foreword
- ◈ Preface
- ◈ Table of Contents

Text

- ◈ Chapters

Back Matter

◈ Conclusion (Afterword/Epilogue)

◈ Appendices

◈ Bibliography/Resources

◈ Glossary

◈ Index

LET'S GET STARTED ON THAT MANUSCRIPT

Most books can be written in 100 – 300 hours. That's uninterrupted time completely dedicated to writing a book. Let's say you are going to write a 70,000-page book and you estimate you can have it done in 200 hours. Take 70,000/200 = 35 pages a week or 35 x 250 = 8,750 words a week. This equates to 1250 words a day.

Next you will want to develop a timeline or writing schedule. In this case you know you can spend two hours a day to write your book. That's 7 days' x 2 hours = 14 hours a week of writing time. At this rate it will take you approximately 8 (at the minimum) – 14.5 weeks (if you take weekends off) to get the book done.

Your next step would be to get a calendar and chart out the desired day and times you will be dedicating to writing the book. You can do this electronically for example in Evernote, in an Excel spreadsheet, or the old fashioned way with a paper calendar and a pen or pencil. I like to set an alarm on my telephone to remind me when I have to start writing on my manuscript. Once you have an established writing schedule, it's time to get busy with the business of writing that manuscript.

Here is one of the popular strategies I share with some of my clients. Before starting to write your first chapter, remember "begin with the end in mind." Nehemiah had envisioned a completed project. That and his faith in God kept him on the wall. Allow the Holy Spirit to be your writing coach. Pray and then get started.

9 STEPS TO WRITING A GREAT MANUSCRIPT

1. Pick two or three possible titles for your book. (They are not set in stone; you can change them at any time. Matter of fact this whole process is very flexible.)

2. Create a Book Vision.

3. Create a Book Mission.

4. Decide on the number of chapters you would like to have.

5. Brainstorm a list of topics you would like to discuss in the book. For fiction writers, it would be a series of events which leads your reader to a dramatic finish. Develop chapter titles for each chapter.

6. Use these topics/event to create chapter titles,

7. Create chapter narratives describe what each chapter is about or the event to take place in each chapter. These narrative should be short paragraphs, 70 to 100 words maximum.

8. Take your chapter narratives and use them as a guide to create content for your chapter. In a nonfiction book it can serve as an introduction. In a fiction novel it can be a catalyst which sparks the creative spirit within.

9. Set a target word count goal for each chapter and start to build your manuscript!

GETTING YOUR MANUSCRIPT READY

If you are interested in traditional publishing do you know how to submit a manuscript or query letter to an agent or publisher for review? Is the format the same for nonfiction and fiction? If you are self-publishing do you need an editor and how much does it cost? *Questions, questions, questions and more questions.* When I had *questions* about my manuscript submission, I was introduced to a wonderful friend at a writer's conference: a book on how to format your manuscript and a lot more titled *Formatting & Submitting Your Manuscript by Chuck Sambuchino and The Editors of Writer's Digest Books.* There are some preliminary steps you need to take before the actual submission of your manuscript. Let's take a look at some of them.

As you research potential traditional publishers, you may find a lot of submission guidelines that say, "no unsolicited manuscripts accepted." In today's publishing industry, an agent is a necessity when you are looking to get your book published.

If you are going that route you will need to:

- ❖ Identify publishers who are interested in the type of book you are publishing by studying other authors in your genre and using the Writer's Market to identify publishers who are looking for books similar to the one you are writing.

- ❖ Do a book proposal. I recommend you do this before you solicit an agent or publisher. In the past this has helped me solidify the direction I wanted to take my book project solicitation and management. I also recommend self-publishing authors complete a proposal for the same reason. A book proposal may be consisting of the following elements:

> A. Cover letter
>
> B. Cover page
>
> C. Overview
>
> D. Marketing information
>
> E. Competitive analysis
>
> F. Author's Bio
>
> G. Chapter Outlines
>
> H. Sample Chapters
>
> I. Any support documentation

Keep in mind the book proposal for a non-fiction book has a different format than a fiction novel. Take your research from the potential publisher's website and create a proposal template which may be easily modified.

◈ Research agents who handle your genre and research their requirements. Ask other authors in your genre and look for online resources which list agents and their specialty areas such as The Writer's Market.

◈ Create a query letter template to solicit agents or editors.

◈ Prepare your manuscript for submission to an agent or editor.

Tips for Submitting Your Manuscript

◈ Become familiar with the market, research, research, and research.

◈ Know what genre your book fits into and look for publishing houses looking for you and agents which specialize in your genre.

◈ FOLLOW SUBMISSION GUIDELINES! Remember you are in competition with hundreds sometimes thousands of other aspiring authors depending on the publishing house. Don't hinder your chances by not meeting the publisher's requirements for submission.

◈ Manuscript formatting is important. I suggest the following:

   » Use plain white paper of a high quality bond paper.

   » Print on only one side of the page.

   » Double space the manuscript.

   » Use Courier or Times New Roman, 12-point type.

   » Use 1" margins on all sides.

- » Indent on the first line of a paragraph.
- » Make sure each page is numbered.
- » Don't include graphics or illustrations unless asked to do so.
- » Don't bind the manuscript.
- » Only send the manuscript electronically if requested by the agent or editor.

Summary

Creating, formatting and submitting your manuscript are some of the most important facets of the AUTHORSHIP journey for authors, especially those desiring a traditional publishing contract. I always say, "Show up, to go up." If you show up in excellence, you can expect excellent results. Do it to the glory of God and you are guaranteed success. Happy Writing!

CHAPTER EIGHT

SEEKING JEHOVAH JIREH

ഏ‍ଓଈ

A fter Nehemiah's plan was approved by the king, his next step was to hire a team of people to help with the project. Even with the king's support many officials opposed the idea.

> *"When I met the governors across The River (the Euphrates) I showed them the king's letters. The king even sent along a cavalry escort. When Sanballat the Horonite and Tobiah the Ammonite official heard about this, they were very upset, angry that anyone would come to look after the interests of the People of Israel." (Nehemiah 2:9-10).*

As an author, you have to become used to the idea not everyone will like your idea. The first publisher/editor you find will probably not see the potential your book has but you can't give up! When Nehemiah was met with opposition, he refused to give up and sought support from the Jews knowing God was by his side.

> "Then I gave them my report: "Face it: we're in a bad way here. Jerusalem is a wreck; its gates are burned up. Come - let's build the wall of Jerusalem and not live with this disgrace any longer." I told them how God was supporting me and how the king was backing me up. They said, "We're with you. Let's get started." They rolled up their sleeves, ready for the good work. When Sanballat the Horonite, Tobiah the Ammonite official, and Geshem the Arab heard about it, they laughed at us, mocking, "Ha! What do you think you're doing? Do you think you can cross the king?" I shot back, "The God-of-Heaven will make sure we succeed. We're his servants and we're going to work, rebuilding. You can keep your nose out of it. You get no say in this - Jerusalem's none of your business!" (Nehemiah 2:17-20).

When we come across obstacles, we as Christians must remember with God on our side, we can move mountains.

> "What, then, shall we say in response to this? **If God is for us, who can be against us?** He who did not spare his own Son, but gave him up for us all--how will he not also, along with him, graciously give us all things? Who will bring any charge against those whom God has chosen? It is God who justifies. Who is he that condemns? Christ Jesus, who died--more than that, who was raised to life--is at the right hand of God and is also interceding for us. [35] Who shall separate us from the love of Christ? Shall trouble or hardship or persecution or famine or nakedness

or danger or sword? ... No, **in all these things we are more than conquerors through him who loved us. For I am convinced that neither death nor life, neither angels nor demons, neither the present nor the future, nor any powers, neither height nor depth, nor anything else in all creation, will be able to separate us from the love of God that is in Christ Jesus our Lord."** *Romans 8:31-39*

HOW TO FINANCIALLY SUPPORT YOUR DREAM

While we are talking about profiting your passion, let me offer you a word of caution. Please don't go and quit your day job without counting the cost to do so. While it is true, there are some very successful people who earn a luxurious living from the books they publish, they represent the exception not the rule. It is also important to note like all writers, they had to first pay their dues.

What is the cost of becoming a writer? If you want to be traditionally published, a PC or Mac with word processing software, a reliable internet service, and your imagination will do in the beginning. Eventually you will want to get a publisher and you may need to acquire an agent to do so. The agent and publisher will need to be wooed by your work and in order to do so you may need to invest in some writer's workshops, attend a few conferences or even hire an editor on your way to being published. It also pays to join some of the more popular national writing groups. One of the best resources for Christian authorpreneurs is The Christian

Writer's Market Guide by Jerry B. Jenkins. It has a Support For Writers section which has a list of Christian writer's workshops and conferences, clubs, fellowship and critique groups, contests, editorial and publicity services, and Christian literary agents. It's well worth the investment.

Other Investments Made By Traditionally Published Authors

When considering the cost of bringing a book from concept to publication, don't forget the time you have invested in this project is valuable. If your present hourly rate is $25, the 240 hours you spend putting together a manuscript compares to a $6000 pay check for services rendered. Also consider the office supplies used, ink cartridges, electricity, cost of Internet service, light bulbs, and the wear and tear on your computer, etc.

Your book may require research. Perhaps you will have to purchase additional reference books on your topic. You may need to make telephone calls a text won't do when you are interviewing a potential expert. Electronic access to media can be a great asset in most cases but if you are a novelist writing historical fiction, you may have to travel to the place you are referencing to do adequate research on that time period. If you are writing a nonfiction book, you may have to travel to discuss your topic with an expert or attend a conference where major thought leaders are discussing it.

Don't forget the costs of commitment money can't buy. What about the time you spend away from your family and friends while completing your writing project? If you run a business how will this compromise the time you are required to invest there? In other words, what are the opportunity costs associated with writing your book?

There are other intrinsic costs: the emotional, mental, and intellectual capital you expend as a result of being on this writer's journey. I salute you for your courage. Now, let's go on a treasure hunt to find that hidden wealth you didn't know was available to you.

Do a Personal Financial Assessment

We have reached a critical juncture. You may need some capital to invest in your literary project. If you are self-publishing, in order to write, edit, publish, market, and distribute your book, you will need some moola, currency, cheddar, or in plain English terms: money. If your goal is to be traditionally published, then your costs will be minimal because the publisher will assume the costs of publishing and marketing the book. Whatever route you have chosen, you must determine what your costs will be and move towards your mark. In the words of Jean-Luc Picard of Star Trek: The Next Generation, "Make it so!"

You must first evaluate your current financial position and determine if you have the extra cash lying around in a shoebox, under your mattress, or hidden in a mysterious safe deposit box somewhere. Wouldn't that be nice? Unfortunately, most people don't.

Before you hire one person on your professional team, be sure to realistically look at your current fiscal responsibilities related to living, medical, transportation, and luxury expenses. Remember long-term costs like your mortgage and short-term debt like credit cards. Can you personally finance this project out of your pocket with your current budget?

If not, you may want to consider looking at some of the following methods:

A. Cut back on some of your luxury expenses such as eating out, getting your nails done, or buying the latest and greatest video games to make those funds available for your book project.

B. Borrow money from family or friends. Please do so with all intentions of paying it back or you may have some miserable holidays as a result.

C. Raise it yourself from personal assets. Such as:

> » Saving Accounts
> » Equity in real estate
> » Retirement Accounts
> » Investments
> » Life Insurance
> » Your 401k or IRA

D. Go on a treasure hunt in your home and office and look for things you have designated as junk you can turn into cash. Such as:

» Broken Gold Jewelry

» Antiques and Family Heirlooms

» Old Coins

» Old Stamp Collections

» Old Books – Collectors Editions

» An Old Car that is Cluttering Up Your Garage

» An Old House that was Left to You By Your Favorite Aunt

» Copper

» Old Appliances

» Etc.

You get the point. The operative word is "old," something you no longer have use for and can live without it.

Now let's look at some other "creative" ways to finance your dream.

◈ Sell some of your witty and creative ideas or inventions.

◈ Use credit card financing, in moderation of course, and only if you're not involved in a get out of debt program. Don't fall off the wagon to publish your book!

◈ Host webinars on topics you are considered an expert on.

◈ Take on a second job or start a home-based business.

◈ Start a publishing company and it will entitle you to several tax deductions for business owners.

◈ Co-publish a book with an experienced author or someone with world or national name recognition.

◈ Co-publish a book with a small press.

◈ Find an unfilled niche and fill it. Look for a local non-profit, business, or organization which shares your passion for a particular cause and join forces with them to get your book published by gifting it to their members, customers, book clubs, or associations.

◈ Crowdfunding or collaborative funding is another option for industrious authorpreneurs who want to get other people to finance your book project. There are two basic models: donations based or investment crowdfunding. In donations based crowdfunding, donors receive a perk or reward for donating something to the campaign. Investment crowdfunding, the person actually invests in your project with the anticipation of a financial return. Some popular crowdfunding websites are Kickstarter, Indiegogo, Patreon, and GoFundMe.

These are all ways you can finance your dream without incurring a huge debt. Now here comes the disclaimer: I am an author not a financial advisor. For more technical assistance please check with a professional.

You may want to look in-the-house before seeking out-of-the-house financing. Let's take a look at what a personal financial assessment may look like:

PERSONAL FINANCIAL SITUATION ASSESSMENT

Select the answer which best fits your financial management style. Mark with an "x: **A** for Always, **S** for Sometimes and **N** for Never. Total the number of responses at the end of each column.

Do you:	A	S	M
Keep an active log of your bank transactions	_____	_____	_____
Have an emergency fund	_____	_____	_____
Use on-line or mobile banking	_____	_____	_____
Have a budget	_____	_____	_____
Comparison shop	_____	_____	_____
Plan for large expenditures such as a car, house, major appliances or a vacation	_____	_____	_____
Set long term and short term financial goals	_____	_____	_____
Only pay cash for your purchases	_____	_____	_____
use credit cards for emergencies only	_____	_____	_____
use credit cards for emergencies only	_____	_____	_____
Total	_____	_____	_____

If the majority of checks are in the:

A – Always   **GREEN LIGHT** – Congratulations, you have excellent personal financial habits.

S – Sometimes   **YELLOW LIGHT** – Proceed with caution! You may need to evaluate some of your spending habits. It's time to get some friendly advice from your local financial advisor.

N – Never   **RED LIGHT – STOP!** Run to your nearest financial institution and tell them you need help or make an appointment with the nearest financial advisor today.

For those of you who desire a more detailed tool to assess your finances, I have created an excellent tool for use and placed it in the Appendix titled *Your Financial Assessment Form.*

Now, let's look at some tools specifically designed for the self-published author. Once you evaluate where you are financially, determine what you want to spend on your book project, establish a budget, and pursue resources which fit your designated budgetary spending. For example, you decide you want to publish and personally finance your book project with money you got from a garage sale, $500. Your budget may look like this:

SERVICE	DESCRIPTION	COSTS
Professional Editing	Developmental, line editing, proofreading	$1500
Interior Layout	Done by a professional or you can buy the software and do-it-yourself	$500
Professional Cover Design	Done by an expert designer who specializes in book cover design	$500
ISBN	International Standard Book Number (10 for $295), the best buy for a publisher (A single ISBN number is $125)	$295
Copyright	On-line	$35 - $55
PCN	Pre-assigned Control Number from the Library of Congress (add an additional $45 to register your copyright)	-0-
Advance Copies	Free books used as promotional copies	$500
Marketing and Promotion	Prior to book launch and at book launch	$1000

Website Design and Creation	Basic without all the frills such as a shopping cart, hosting, and domain name purchase, and SEO optimization.	$1500
Visual and Graphics Design	Photography, logo design, and other elements that go into your marketing kit and on your website	$500
TOTAL COSTS		**$6350.00**

There is however a less costly way to publish. If you want to test the waters before you make a sizable investment in your book project, you may want to publish an e-book version. Your budget may look like this:

SERVICE	DESCRIPTION	COST
E-Book Formatting	Turning your word document into e-book format	$200
Editor	Checking for grammar, punctuation, and spelling.	$800
Cover Design	Turning your cover design into e-book format	$125
ISBN	A block of 10 numbers	$295

E-Book Publisher	Self-publishing, on-demand printing, and online distribution services (Upgraded Services)	$100
	TOTAL COSTS	**$1520.00**

Summary

After assessing your personal financial position and deciding exactly which road is most cost effective for your budget, you are ready for the next step writing God inspired manuscript that is going to change the world.

CHAPTER NINE

FINDING THE PEOPLE WHO HAVE A HEART TO WORK

So we built the wall and the whole wall was joined together to half its height, for the people had a mind to work. Nehemiah 4:6

God commissioned Nehemiah to do the work but his next task after convincing King Artaxerxes to champion his cause was to convince the people of Israel to actually rebuild the wall. The key to his success in doing so was God turning the heart of the people to support the mission. He presented his case and the people embraced the cause. Everything he needed was within the broken walls of Jerusalem.

Likewise, anyone on your team will need to have a mind to work and successfully complete the task based on your book's mission. Nehemiah could not do it alone and neither can you.

Are You Part of a Winning TEAM?

If you have not yet figured it out, I was a child with a vivid imagination and television was a major contributor to my fantasy world. Even today when I am in a room with a television, it is very hard to get my attention. The sad thing is my siblings suffer from the same malady. I was particularly fond of westerns when I was a child because I always wanted the "good guy" to win. One of my favorite shows was The Lone Ranger, a television western about a masked Texas Ranger who fought injustice on the old western frontier that which entertained audiences from 1949 to 1957. The Lone Ranger wore a "white hat" like all good guys did in westerns and he always got his man. Sometimes this required the help of his faithful Indian friend Tonto, so The Lone Ranger was not truly alone.

Unfortunately, some authors start their literary journey solo. Perhaps cost is a factor or they may be overly optimistic about their abilities to "DIY" alone. As a seasoned author, I advise you to take the path of The Lone Ranger and have a trusted companion to ride out this literary journey with you. In this case an advisory team of support professionals may cost you a little money up front, but will save you tons of money on the back end.

The Team Makes The Dream Work!

"How does one transform a life? By reaching deep inside and pulling up courage and creativity. Who does that better than a writer? A writer is one who sits at a desk day in and day out digging dip into their spirit for the voice of the muse, but it takes a village for

a writer to become an author. Manuscripts require a community. Think of all the people who contribute to a book's final outcome: an agent; writing coach; an editor; graphics designer; a traditional, digital or self-publisher; good friends; and more.

Writers love to tell their stories. They tell the story of how they wrote their books, the content of it, and about their writing processes. That's what makes everyone fall in love with him or her. Everyone loves a good story. Every community needs to have regular book readings by authors and organizations which support writers. They are the fresh breath of what we take in so we can then emulate them in being courageous, creative, and transform our own stories." Jan Marquart, Author of Kate's Way

For years, I wrote poetry and only shared it with a few trusted friends and family members. It wasn't until I was challenged to read it before an audience of writers I realized my work was so much bigger than I was and the world was interested, but I would have to be more professional in my delivery. I started taking acting classes. In those classes, I found my next great love, speaking. For years, I would write poetry and perform it on stage. As I perfected my craft, I began to get requests to do presentations all over the city of Detroit. You might say "good for you," but I was not so thrilled at the time. That's not my calling. At the time, I did not feel I was called to the stage either, I shook in my boots every time I did a presentation. Still, I went on to perform and learned what true courage was. I only accomplished this with the help of a team. My drama coach, support of my family and friends, and mentors were instrumental in my achieving the success which resulted from my staying the course, and as Joyce Meyer says, "doing it afraid."

As a closeted writer, I would have been content occasionally jotting down a word here or there and showing it sheepishly to a close-knit group of fans. I was safe there and rejection was minimal, but if I'd not taken that step of faith and gotten the help and support I needed, I honestly would not be writing this book today. I embraced my call because others validated me by coming alongside to help me reach my ultimate destination. God knew I would need a "village" to raise me to the heights He was taking me to and as always in His infinite wisdom; He orchestrated a plan for me to walk in His highest good for my life.

Writers are a solitary lot. It's comfortable behind our pen, but "If I write it then they will come" is not a realistic expectation in this season for authors. The competition for the hearts of readers is fierce. They are sensationalized, anesthetized, frightened out of their wits, immortalized and seduced daily by content which only gives them a temporary fix. You have an obligation to equip yourself for the modern day playing field because you have a calling to bring quality writing back to the forefront of the book storefront. So, let's look at some practical reasons for building a winning support team.

Let's start with your relational support team, those in your inner-circle who render help at the drop of a text or phone call. When my children were little, my Little Black Book consisted of phone numbers for potential babysitters because if you have children occasionally you will need the support of a babysitter. Then there are those friends and family you can count on to give you honest feedback on what you've written no matter what. These are the people you know love you, but ain't (excuse my slang) afraid to tell you the truth. In my case, it's my first born who I respect because he is very practical, wise beyond his years and doesn't mind sharing his opinion in love. For creative folks like us it brings balance to our book project.

Speaking of balance, all work and no play makes you a schizophrenic writer. Having a support team will allow you to spend more time with the people you love like your family, friends, and fellow pew warmers. In the words of Hillary Rodham Clinton, "Don't confuse having a career, with having a life."

I was invited to a friend's house to preview his manuscript. He was a former runner for the mob and a casino manager in Las Vegas and is now a born-again believer who shares his testimony with everyone he meets. There were nine of us gathered together to accomplish this task including the ghostwriter. He is writing about his exploits on the way to his spiritual "promised land."

I mention his event because I learned so much about his life that I hadn't previously known because I love him so much as a friend, I actually hurt because his journey sometimes seemed so hopeless. In addition to fighting those battles, he has had Crohn's disease most of his adult life. Watching his life turn towards Christ as he told his story reminded me again of the vital importance of the written word. His life story will be extremely relevant in today's world as an evangelistic tool for other seemingly hopeless individuals. I left that experience proud of my contribution and amazed at his courage to tell the whole truth of his journey.

I've also found it very valuable to consult fellow writers. I've built relationships with writers all over the country as a result of my radio show and conferences. and can find someone in any genre to render advice for FREE, simply because I've spent time getting to know them and celebrating their talents. Now, let's look at the professional side of building a support team.

Consulting seasoned professionals will not only save you money but also time. One of the things writers fail to do when they put pen to paper is consider their personal investment in the writing of their book. For example, if someone hired you to write a book, how much would you charge him or her per hour and how long would you estimate it would take you to complete the project? Once you've calculated your proposed asking price, attribute that same cost to the completion of your book and you will gain an added appreciation for seeking the counsel of others on this project.

Rarely will a businessperson start an entrepreneurial endeavor without at least an attorney and a CPA to assist them in the startup of their business. Yet, every day someone sits down to write a book without the counsel of anyone and ends up spinning their wheels instead of moving their project forward because they decided to do things as Frank Sinatra said he did in his song, "I did it my way!" Let's make it relate to Generation Z. You may be tempted to—in the words of Burger King— "Have it your way!" Remember, "Plans fail for lack of counsel, but with many advisers they succeed."(Proverbs 15:22)

Writing a book makes you an instant businessperson. A book becomes an entity of its own once completed. It has a name, ISBN number, Library of Congress Catalog Number, assigned value, and groupies (book clubs). Like a corporation, it takes on a separate personality from its originator and acquires more worth as other people invest in it. Therefore, you should approach your project as the primary stakeholder in its success with a business mindset.

When you establish an advisory team of support professionals, your team could look like this:

Editor —An editor reviews what you have written and makes recommendations on the general strengths and weaknesses of your manuscript. For example, an editor reviews writing mechanics such as grammar, punctuation, syntax, and language for your intended niche.

Publicist —A publicist is a person responsible for publicizing your book.

Agent —An agent is a person who represents you in the business, contractual, or management of your book.

Literary Coach —A person who specializes in motivating, training, and advising you through the completion of your book.

Writers Group —A group of people who help you perfect the craft of writing frequently segregated by genre.

Attorney (Intellectual Property) —An individual who specializes in intellectual property. They may help you register a copyright or review a publisher's contract.

Accountant —This individual will assist you in keeping track of financials related to your book and complete your business taxes.

Publisher —The entity which produces, distributes, markets and sells your book.

Tips On Selecting Your Support Team

- ◈ Interview Prospects
- ◈ Look for people who understand your mission and vision for the book
- ◈ Review their credentials and ask for references
- ◈ Research average costs for these services in your particular geographical area
- ◈ Query your professional network for recommendations
- ◈ Once you do your research on the prices of these services rendered by your team, stick to your allocated budget
- ◈ Conduct a minimum of one group meeting with all the members of your support team
- ◈ Schedule regular meetings as needed with your team, individually or collectively based on their availability. Skype,

FreeConferenceCall.com, or Google Hangouts are great free tools readily available for your use to accomplish this task.

◈ Use your team as a resource to assist you in acquiring endorsements, your foreword, editorial contributions, etc.

Tips On Managing Your Advisory Support Team

◈ Clarity – Are the members of your team clear about your vision for your book? Do they understand your overall goals and objectives for your literary project? As the leader of the group, you must ensure everyone on board has a keen understanding of what you are trying to accomplish with your book.

◈ Comprehension – Before you solicit team members, you must be clear about what role they will play on the team and share it with them during the recruitment process and also during the course of the project. Having a definitive job description for each member will bring clarity to the team and keep you on track during the research and development phase. I am reminded of Cuba Gooding Jr. re-educating Tom Cruise in the movie *Jerry Maguire* of what his role was as his manager. "Show me the money!" he told him. Well, you have to be specific about your expectations for your team members and lead by example in order to have a successful book project.

◈ Consistency – If a team member is too busy to participate in the process on a regular basis, frankly, they are too busy to bring the necessary intellectual capital required for you to have a successful finish. You, as the leader of the team, must model this mode of operation and also expect your team members to "bring it" when they are required to do so.

◈ Care – One of my favorite quotes from President Theodore Roosevelt is "People don't care how much you know until they know how much you care." People come to a project and stay with a project because they care about the cause, the person, or the expected outcome. If you show them you care about them by celebrating their involvement, you'll be able to conquer the world. At the end of the project, throw a party for your team and celebrate your magnificent achievement.

◈ Collaborate – A prudent business minded individual uses all the resources available. It is not unthinkable to recruit individuals to volunteer their time on your advisory team. You are worth the investment; however, you may need to sell them on the intrinsic benefits associated with being part of a winning team. Make sure you mention them in the acknowledgements and thank them profusely when the project is finished. Also, bartering is not out of the question. You are an expert in something or you would not be writing a book. Use that expertise to collaborate with someone who needs what you offer and who is willing to do an intellectual capital exchange.

Earlier, we discussed the relational team and professional team. Make a list of those who are already on your team that is rendering support and send them a thank you card, take them to lunch, or throw a party in their honor. Acknowledge your gratitude for their investment in your life by celebrating them.

Review the Support Team Evaluation Form for your professional support team. I recommend you at least do a quarterly evaluation of your progress. Remember, your initial purpose for having a support team is to get it done with excellence. Don't compromise, super-size your book project!

Summary

I've given you quite a bit to think about in this chapter but you are up to the challenge. If Nehemiah can rebuild Jerusalem, you can write your book. Remember the challenges men and women have overcome *as a team* with God on their side. Remember the brave escapades of The Lone Ranger and garner strength from his unshakeable courage. "A fiery horse with the speed of light, a cloud of dust and a hearty 'Hi-Yo Silver!' Away!" The Lone Ranger rides again! (By the way Tonto was right there by his side.)

CHAPTER TEN

BE MISSION FOCUSED
AND BATTLE READY

℘℘℘

Now that you've developed your strategic plan, accounting for obstacles you might run into and gathered your team together, completing your book project can be intimidating. Some writers will never make it past the planning stage because they are so caught up in the enormity of the task they have before them. Just like folding laundry, you do the job one item at a time.

The best thing you can do as a writer is just WRITE. Don't worry about the other facets of getting your manuscript ready quite yet. You do want to keep in mind who your audience is and where you want your book to go, but don't try to edit as you write. Sidney Sheldon once said that "a blank piece of paper is God's way of telling us how hard it is to be God." Many writers never get their book published because they have the "idea" in their head already and to write it down will in their minds ruin the story. So instead of writing, using bad grammar, and poor characterization the writers get lost never making it past chapter one, editing each sentence until they have it "perfect." Instead, follow Nehemiah's example and be mission focused and battle ready.

Another thing to keep in mind is to never give up. When you feel writer's block setting in or the naysayers descending, the little voice in your head saying you're not a real author, pray. When the local officials mocked the rebuilding process and even tried to disrupt it by using force, this is what the headline on the Nehemiah Gazette looked like the next day, "*We countered with prayer to our God and set a round-the-clock guard against them*" *(Nehemiah 4:9).*

You can't become so attached to your plan you don't know how to adapt to obstacles and therefore stop working. When the officials started attacking the building crews Nehemiah adapted to the circumstances putting lances in the crew's hands. (Nehemiah 4:13-16)

The key point about Nehemiah's story is he never stopped working. He was threatened, accused of treason, and nearly assassinated, but he didn't stop until the wall was finished. We must remember with God on our side, success is ours as long as we continue moving forward. Even if it means you only write two sentences a day, those two sentences mean you fought against all of the obstacles telling you to stop and they proclaim God is with you and helping you.

In this chapter, you will find lots of tools to help you follow Nehemiah's example and manage your time effectively.

TIME MANAGEMENT

An Authorpreneur is a sole proprietor of sorts. You are a one person "mean writing machine" with best-seller stars in your eyes and a pen in your hand. In other words, you are your own boss and your only employee. As a writer, it may mean holding yourself accountable to meet deadlines and honor a mandatory self-imposed daily word count in order to finish your manuscript on time.

Unfortunately, there is a common flaw which seems inherent to those skilled with ink and pen. Procrastination. For some writers this tendency is due to the business of living. Deadlines take a backseat to everything else. In addition, there are other tasks required of you as an Authorpreneur that must get done in conjunction with writing. So how can you successfully navigate life and work? Let's take an honest look at some tips you can incorporate into your life to "git er done" (a common Texas slang for getting the job accomplished).

Writing is your job. Be it fulltime or part-time; make it the #1 priority for that season of your life. You would not tell your boss you couldn't finish your presentation for an important client because you had to watch your favorite television show. Get rid of the clutter in your life-- and which includes habits or routines that hinder your progress to honor your commitment and "git er done."

Evaluate your time management skills by taking the **Writers Time Management Test** and set a baseline for your "git er done" improvement plan. You can improve what you can measure.

Writers Time Management Test

Directions: Circle each statement in Part One and Part Two of the time management test that is currently a time management habit. Give yourself 2 points for each of the following habits you have.

Part One: How Well Do I "Git er Done"?

1. I make a "TO DO" list every day, prioritizing the most important things at the top of that list and carrying over those things which did not get done to the next day's list.

2. I have a daily calendar I use to keep track of my scheduled activities and writing deadlines.

3. I have a weekly calendar I use to keep track of my scheduled activities and writing deadlines.

4. I have a monthly calendar I use to keep track of my scheduled activities and writing deadlines.

5. When I hit "overwhelm," I take a break from my work area and come back refreshed and invigorated.

6. I schedule my availability to answer telephone calls or respond to e-mails around my writing schedule so I can have uninterrupted quality writing time.

7. I use the electronic time management tools available to me on my cell phone and or computer.

8. I use sticky notes to remind me of what must be accomplished daily.

9. I am not afraid to delegate tasks to others.

10. I boldly seek out the resources I need and make time for the necessary research in order to lend credibility to my work.

11. I have identified my best working atmosphere and have taken steps to create a sanctuary so there are no hindrances in my writing environment.

12. I know where the calculator, calendar, and word count function are on my computer so I can do my work faster.

13. I have identified when I am most alert and I schedule my time to write accordingly.

14. I use the sandwich principle. I schedule the tasks I don't like to do between the tasks I do like, so I am inspired to work faster to get to the tasks I enjoy.

15. I have a budget to manage my money.

16. I am in good health.

17. I get enough rest, exercise, and eat healthy foods.

18. I constantly review my short and long term goals to make sure I'm on track to best seller status.

19. I keep God, family, and friends as a priority in this process not forgetting their importance in my life and striving for balance by not making unwise sacrifices to "git er done."

20. I realize "stuff happens" and I am flexible enough in my plan to can make the necessary adjustments when it does.

TOTAL POINTS, PART ONE: _____

Part Two: What Prohibits Me From "Gittin er done?"

1. I am so fascinated with social media I would rather spend my time on Facebook, Pinterest, LinkedIn, or Instagram.

2. I have over 5,000 unread emails I'm waiting until my next vacation to read them all because I am afraid I might miss something.

3. As a generalist, I master of a lot of things, but I like it that way because I can write about anything and I spend a lot of time doing research so when I get ready to write my book, I can write a book that can reach everybody.

4. I use my "wait" time while at the doctor's office and other places to wait for something to happen. After all, a little relaxation has never hurt anyone. Some people call it laziness; I call it conserving my energy for the next BIG opportunity.

5. I am a perfectionist and everything must be perfect before I can move forward on a project.

6. I have too many responsibilities which prohibit me from committing to anything for any length of time.

7. Everyone needs me on his or her team. I'm so critical to their mission their organization would come to a complete stop if I didn't volunteer. You've heard of the 20/80 rule; 20% of the people do 80% of the work. I'm part of the 20%.

8. I must keep my mobile phone close to me at all times because people are always trying to contact me. I might miss an important text, news item, Facebook post, or call. I check it every ten minutes, I feel lost without it.

9. Before I can write, I need some kind of inspiration. I often sit for hours waiting for my muse to visit me.

10. I enjoy writing so much, I write about everything and everywhere. I've got 50 boxes of stuff I wrote packed away in my garage. One day, I'm going to put it all into a book. Everybody tells me I should write one. I'm already halfway there; I just need to organize my garage to find everything.

11. I usually don't wake up until noon. I'm a night person and I party or watch TV until the wee hours of the morning. I need my social time, it's a priority in my life.

12. My work schedule is so overwhelming, I don't have time to do much else, much less plan my day or prioritize my tasks.

13. I just can't multitask. I can only do one thing at a time.

14. Yes, I am a couch potato and proud of it. I need to watch TV to unwind from my day when I come home from work. It keeps me sane and my spouse happy.

15. I am a habitual worrier, it takes up a lot of my time and causes me to have many restless nights, but I just can't help it.

16. Being organized is not one of my strong suits. I can never find anything but nobody's perfect.

17. I keep everything in my head. I don't need a calendar.

18. I take a break every chance I get especially since they aren't paying me what I'm worth.

19. I often take personal calls at work and I have frequent visitors. It helps my day go by faster.

20. My schedule is so chaotic. I can never seem to get it together, no matter how hard I try. I'm always double-booked and late for appointments and deadlines. I think I need a virtual assistant.

TOTAL POINTS, PART TWO:_____

FINAL SCORE: Subtract Part Two from Part One

Part One Points:

Part Two Points:

TOTAL:

What your final score means:

If you score between 30 and 40, you are excellent at managing your time. Feel free to write a book on Time Management.

If you score between 19 and 29, your time management skills are average. Periodically study the suggestions in Part One to either improve or maintain your time management skills.

If you score below 18, you really need to concentrate on improving your time management skills. The best way to fight procrastination is to maximize your ability to manage the time allotted to a task.

This may take some practice on your part but it will be well worth the effort. Remember, consistency is key; do something for 21 days and it becomes a habit.

Now that you know the baseline score for your time management skills, let's discuss some standard tips to assist you in being a good steward of your time.

When developing your time management strategies, you should consider the following:

1. Self-control – I remember the first time I saw the fruit of the Spirit in Galatians; the only one I had an immediate challenge with was self-control. I was a babe in Christ with spiritual milk still behind my ears and I wrestled with the concept self-discipline was a part of the evidence that God was at work in my life.

   As a Powerful Choleric, I love to be in control but I don't like to be controlled even by myself. As a writer, it is my desire to please God as an act of gratitude for the gift he has given me. My love for God pushed me over my discomfort and I recognized the valuable fruits self-control brought into my life as a result.

   The same principle applies to writing. It may be a little uncomfortable for a season when making the necessary changes listed in Part One of the Writers Time Management Test but the fruit of your efforts are guaranteed to result in a more excellent book.

2. Prioritizing – Life has a way of setting priorities for you if you don't set them yourself. Take a realistic look at what's going on in your life and identify the time robbers, the things which keep you from doing the things that mean the most and develop a plan to eradicate them.

   Next make a list of your short, medium, and long term goals. Don't forget to incorporate the dream sheet you filled out in Chapter One. Divide the list into three categories: *Short-Term Goals, Medium Goals, and Long-Term Goals* then prioritize them based on their importance to you and the God purpose for your life.

   Review your short-term goals weekly, medium-term goals monthly and your long term goals quarterly. Incorporate the *Reveal, Revisit, and Realign* Principle in your reviewing process to stay on top of any changes you may need to make based on the God factor which often influences the trajectory of our lives. In other words, make a commitment to do the work to define your short-term goals and reveal them to all of your stakeholders, revisit them on a regularly scheduled basis, and realign when necessary.

   Goals help you stay focused on the prize. Maintaining your focus breeds productivity and productivity gives you a sense of accomplishment. What writer isn't happy when they complete the last page of the last chapter of a book?

3. Balance – Writing should be a part of your life. It should never be your life. Sometimes finding a balance between life

and writing is hard but incorporating a schedule is the best remedy for that.

Make time for God, family, friends and you a priority. It eliminates the guilt and over compensation you experience when you neglect your loved ones and the break in fellowship with your Heavenly Father may cost you more than you are willing to pay. My relationship with God strengthens my reserve to complete the task at hand. I am empowered to do the impossible because He is my muse and I firmly believe I can do all things because of Him even thwart my arch enemy, *Procrastination* and you can too!

If you don't factor time for rest and recreation into your life, you won't be able to refuel for the writing task at hand. This is critical because you are the major common denominator in the formula for your writing success.

Relationships are the fuel which keep you moving towards the completion of your goals. Once you successfully complete them, you want to make sure there is someone there to celebrate with.

4. Flexibility – The only time a person should be rigid is when they are a corpse. You don't want them to put on your tombstone ... *They lived, they wrote, and they died. The End!* Be nice to yourself by allowing the stuff that happens to do just that, happen and then accept it and move on. What writer has never had a manuscript mysteriously disappear into cyberspace when working on a deadline or wrote a beautiful

passage and had to delete it because it lacked relevance to the overall premise? A temporary delay does not mean a permanent detour from your writing goals. Pick up that pen and begin again.

5. Help –"I give you all the credit, God—
   you got me out of that mess,
   you didn't let my foes gloat.
   God, my God, I yelled for help
   and you put me together.
   God, you pulled me out of the grave,
   gave me another chance at life ..." Psalm 30:1 -3a

David was a man after God's own heart, he was so transparent with God. There are numerous stories in the Old Testament where he was in trouble and he called upon God for the help he needed. Authors should not be afraid to let their request be known to the significant people in their lives.

Read my lips, "It is okay to ask for help when you need it." Share your writing schedule with family and friends. Some of the best motivators are teenagers. They love the role reversal and are some of the best dictators around.

Another alternative is to hire an accountability coach. That's what I do for my clients and we have an awesome love-hate relationship. I develop a writing schedule for them and hold them to it. When they hold their precious book baby in their hands for the first time, they forgive me and sing my praises to everyone they meet.

One of my clients is a very successful local marketing expert and she'd never considered writing a book until she heard me do a workshop on *Establishing Yourself As An Expert Through Writing*. I mentioned in my talk that a book was the new business card for entrepreneurs. She caught the vision and asked me to help her. She had a special challenge which had prohibited her from writing for years, she was dyslexic. Once she decided to do it, she wanted it done in 45 days. I developed a schedule for her and did a substantive edit on her manuscript. She turned it over to her copy editor and met her deadline. Now, she goes around telling people about how marvelous I am and I get free publicity whenever she tells her story.

The moral of this story is, if you ask, they will come. So ask for help. In the words of the Nike slogan: *"Just Do It!"* If you are a little squeamish learn the lyrics of the song *"Help!"* and sing it to your potential rescuer if that's what it takes. Do whatever you have to do to get the help you need, just don't let pride stand in the way, of asking for help.

If you incorporate the above suggestions, you will be well on your way to mastering time management. Gaining awareness of the things which prohibit you from reaching your writing goals is priceless. It is important to stay on the course until the book is completed.

Deadlines are an important part of the publication process. Being proactive versus reactive in accomplishing them allows you the privilege of mastering the balancing act of living a fulfilled life in the midst of answering your call to write. You possess all you need to do so.

Implementing these time management skills may require some additional soul searching and prayer but it will all be worth it in the end and your readers win because they get a chance to pick up a great book with your name on it.

WRITERS BLOCK

"Who is more to be pitied, a writer bound and gagged by policemen or one living in perfect freedom who has nothing more to say?"
—— Kurt Vonnegut

Writers block is the infectious pox of a writer with a deadline. If you have ever desired to write anything of great importance and been behind schedule, it probably has tried to pull you off course and derail all your attempts to communicate your message to the masses by sabotaging your manuscript. If it rears its ugly head before the completion of your manuscript, pray my sister, pray my brother!

Sometimes the fountain runs dry, the inkwell empties, words stop coming, or the characters stop talking to you and well the diagnosis is fairly simple, you have writers block. There are several things you can do about it as I mentioned above prayer works. Or take a trip, go get your favorite ice cream, go to the movies, to a comedy show, do an arts and crafts project, change your geography, read a magazine, look at your favorite television show (a personal favorite), or just write badly until you can return to normalcy. Remember weeping may endure for a night (your editor's) but JOY cometh in the morning. Wait on the sunrise that's enough inspiration for anyone.

BRANDING

Back in the old "Wild Wild West" it was customary to mark cattle with a branding iron to signify ownership. A cow's identity was easily distinguishable once the brand was applied to his hide. Now we are not going to resort to those measures to establish a value added brand for you but we are going to take a closer look at how people view you and your anticipated literary project.

A brand in today's vernacular is the technique or means by which you promote your product or service. Specifically, it's the image you project to the world but you want this image to be authentic a true representation of "you."

"In this ever-changing society the most powerful and enduring brands are built from the heart. They are real and sustainable. Their foundations are stronger because they are built with the strength of the human spirit not an ad campaign. The companies lasting are those that are authentic."
—— Howard Schultz, *Pour Your Heart Into It: How Starbucks Built a Company One Cup at a Time*

The spin doctors in Hollywood are great at spinning an image for actors and actresses. Frequently if you get to really know these people, you find out that they are very different from the characters they play. In the literary world it is distinctly different. NEWSFLASH!!! My dear sisters and brothers, you are going to have to come from behind your Apple iPad or PC and face the real world because they really want to know you.

Merriam-Webster's online dictionary defines branding as: *the promoting of a product or service by identifying it with a particular brand.*

Here's a formula for book selling success: THE AUTHENTIC YOU + BRAND + CONSUMER RELATIONSHIP = BOOK SALES

Joanna Penn in *Branding for Writers: An Essential step to Building Your Author Platform* defined branding as "Effectively understanding your own purpose, that of your audience, and the ways to connect the two. That's it, just a word to describe a much deeper and more meaningful process."

Your reading audience is hungry for more of you. They love your books and want to develop a more intimate relationship with the author; this develops reader loyalty and a fan base like Joel Osteen's. That's the "why" of this chapter. So if your self-image needs polishing, now is the time to do it.

Let's start by examining "you" to determine your brand.

◈ What is your genre specialty? If you write in more than one genre, what hooks them together? For example: Are all of your books about a historical time period or are they all about females in distress?

◈ What's your story? Why did you pick up the pen to write? What motivated you to tell a story or share your expertise?

◈ Define the prominent message in your writing? For example: Always follow the golden rule. "Do unto others as you would have them do unto you."

◈ Who are you writing for? Who is your target market?

◈ When a reader picks up your book, how do you want them to see you as the writer behind their reading experience? What is your writing signature?

◈ If you had to pick something tangible to describe your brand as a writer what would it be? For example: What color, animal, single descriptive word, or image best represents your writing style?

◈ Who are your writing mentors and how have they influenced your writing style? What is your "why" for admiring and respecting their work? How do you incorporate it into your writing?

You may want to ask a close friend these questions to see what kind of image you are projecting to them. Knowledge is power and there's nothing like the constructive criticism of someone near to you to help generate necessary change.

On a professional note before you ask yourself: "What image do I want the world to see when they see me?" You should ask yourself: "What is my personal marketability?" Look in the mirror and evaluate your assets as an individual. Your face, voice, body, and ability to articulate both the spoken and the written word will be part of the marketing package which sells your book. Authors often hide behind their pen and choose to project a mysterious persona. In today's publishing industry, it's all about the marketing package which includes little old you.

People sometimes make a careful decision to buy your book not on its contents but on who or what they see on the cover. When Harold Robbins writes a book and places his name on the cover, his reputation dictates it will be a good read. On the other hand if Charlie Sheen were to write a book about his adventures on Two and a Half Men, people may buy it out of curiosity.

That's why tabloids are so popular; readers are seduced by the sensationalism. The entertainment industry makes trillion of dollars selling "hype." Good news, bad news, it doesn't matter what type it is, what matters is that it is available to pacify our insatiable appetite for being in the know. So you must determine what your public persona is going to be. The good news is you can engineer an authentic brand best suitable for your book. The bad news is if you don't the world will do it for you.

Don't let the world tell you who you are, establish your own brand by marketing your exceptionality, your niche. The thing which makes you special! You've done that by answering the questions above.

Once this is identified use it when deciding on your author's photo, the style and design of your website, and your social media profiles such as Facebook, LinkedIn, and Twitter. This should also be considered when you create your logo, business cards, and any promotional media. Everything you create should be consistent with whatever you determine will be your brand.

Now we have talked about what you should do to establish your brand, let's talk about what you should not do. Thou shalt not:

- ❖ Lie - Do not assume the position of the spin doctors and give the people what you think they want. Give them the authentic you. That is the springboard for success. A fabricated image requires a lot of maintenance. Just be you, and that will do!

- ❖ Dance between two opinions – In this business you must be definitive about who you are and what you write about. Otherwise you are in the people pleasing business and that's not what writing is all about. Writing is about having a voice to say the things only you can say in a manner only you can say them in. There are readers who are looking for that voice and if you brand yourself properly, they will find you.

- ❖ Forget to place a guard over your mouth – Social media allows you the privilege of getting your message to the masses instantaneously. Be very careful what you post and where you post it online. You must have a social media plan.

This will require you to develop a strategy for generating communications which build your writing platform. Do the work and evaluate where and what social media medium is best for you. Also use this same advice when developing any promotional materials from post cards to your "About the Author." Your brand is a precious commodity, protect and care for it like it's your first born.

◈ Use vain repetitions – Are you an emailing, tweeting, or Facebook maniac? Does more represent greater exposure to you thus more customers? Be careful you are not compromising your brand by post overload. Eventually people will begin to ignore you and that defeats your overall purpose. Quality versus quantity is the question here. As an expert or tantalizing teaser, you should only speak when you have something valuable to contribute to the conversation, online or in person. That' all I have to say about that.

◈ Try to possess the land not promised to you – God had a specific geographical "promised land" for His people. Identify yours and stay within its boundaries. Who are the major thought leaders or influencers who can help you grow and expand your readership territory within your genre? Identify them and build your social media platforms accordingly. Find out where your target market hangs out and strategically place yourself in their midst. Being everywhere is virtually impossible and being everything to everyone is exhausting. Don't devalue your brand by trying to do either of these things, it's a waste of time and time is something you don't want to waste.

◈ Forget the benefits of the Old Testament – There are critical principles in the Old Testament which help us live a more victorious life today. The stories remind us of perseverance, undying faith, and give us a true example of the reverential fear of God. Just like in the Old Testament, there are still traditional means that can benefit you when developing your brand such as face to face, group communications, and real world relationships. Couple those with the social media tools and you have a winning plan.

◈ Forget that wisdom is found in a multitude of counselors – You may possess numerous talents and skills but there are still some areas you have not mastered. In this day and age of "do it yourself," don't over extend yourself. Get the necessary help you need in order to produce a quality product. If that requires you hiring a coach, taking classes, hiring a graphics designer, web developer, social media consultant, or a videographer do it because you have a vested interest in excellence. Not doing so could compromise your brand and put you back in the book of Genesis at the beginning.

◈ Forget to take an account of your good measure blessing – Now that you've implemented a plan to build your brand you can sit back and watch it work for the rest of your life. Wrong, being blessed with success requires accountability. Periodically you have to step back and measure your progress. How will you know your plan has sustaining power unless you evaluate its success against your short and long term goals? For example: When measuring the effectiveness of an email campaign targeted towards a certain market in several geographical areas, you can use Constant Contact's analytics to measure the opens in each of those areas. If you want to measure the traffic on your website, try Google Analytics. There are also several tools available for you to measure your personal metrics such as onlineIDCalculator.com and lithium.com. Take a few moments and check these out and remember you are already blessed and highly favored, count on it!

Your next step is to check out your competition. God made you unique, no one in this universe has fingerprints exactly the same but you still have two thumbs. In other words, being similar is relevant.

In order to firmly establish your "only one of its kind" brand ask yourself the following questions:

- ◈ Is there a best-selling author with a similar brand? You don't want to be branded as a "copycat."
- ◈ How are other authors in my genre' showcasing their exceptionality?
- ◈ How do other authors use their brand on their marketing materials?
- ◈ Where do I see authors in my genre' marketing their products?
- ◈ What marketing products are they using to get the word out about their books?

◈ What are readers saying in their book reviews about my competition?

◈ What types of promotions draw readers to my competition?

◈ What does a best-selling author in my genre' look like?

◈ How are they using social media to establish their author platform?

Branding Your Book

In the previous section we focused quite a bit of time focusing on building your author platform, now we will spend some time discussing how to brand your book. Let's start on the inside. Writing for the sake of writing does not brand your book.

Your fiction content should be entertaining and well written holding your reader captive until the end. Your non-fiction content should be informative, instructional, inspirational and motivational. Hiring a professional and experienced editor to do line/or structural editing to ensure your inside is as great as your book cover is a worthy investment. If you are looking to be traditionally published, this will help you "sell" your agent or publisher on your manuscript. If you are self-publishing, this is an absolute necessity because the quality of your end product is a direct representation of you.

Now let's look at the book's cover. Frequently this is your first point of contact with a potential reader. It is recommended you incorporate the KISS Principle (Keep It Simple Sweetie) when you select your cover design. Seek the assistance of an experienced designer to assist you in selecting colors, tones, fonts and graphics.

Your book title is also an important piece of the book cover puzzle. Mimic the advertising strategies used in Fortune 500 companies across the nation by creating an attention getting, catchy title that will grip your potential readers from across a crowded bookstore. For example: the word "tissues" has been replaced by "Kleenex" because the Kimberly-Clark Corporation did a great job of branding their product when they first introduced it in 1924 and continued to do so for 89 years. Consistency is the key to successfully branding any product, including your book. A copyeditor can assist you in putting a professional spin on that product.

All support tools such as your website, promotional materials, social media pages and print media such as flyers, postcards, business cards, and press kit (design and content) should reinforce your brand.

Register the domain name for your title and author name. On your website showcase, reader testimonials, book reviews, news clippings, press releases, your bio, and a book trailer. Include a copy of your book cover, excerpts, and an alluring synopsis.

Establishing social media pages for your book or you as an author is your next step. Such as on:

◈ Facebook
◈ LinkedIn

- Pinterest
- Twitter
- Instagram
- YouTube
- TikToc
- Goodreads, etc.

Some tools used to maintain these pages:

- HootSuite
- Buffer
- CoSchedule
- Edgar
- Crowdfire
- iContact
- Sprout Social
- TweetDeck
- TweetChat, etc.

Once you have your book brand solidified be sure to market and build relationships with like-minded people.....Sell a lot of books!

As you develop your story, remember the authors that have mastered branding like Joel Osteen: who is known for positive reinforcement, Stephen King: Horror, Karen Kingsbury: Christian tear-jerkers with strong, characters, family dynamics and lots of emotion. WOW! This is branding. Your work may precede you but readers with inquiring minds really want to know you because you are connected at the intersection of your purpose and theirs.

I witnessed an astonishing event at a book festival. I was in a room with a male author who gave a dramatic reading of a chapter in his book. The room was full of book clubs and the readers (mostly women) were well versed in his series of books. They spoke intelligently about his characters and their love for his writing style but when he opened his mouth to read they were mesmerized. Then he sang at the request of one of the ladies and you could hear a pen drop in the room. That's the miracle of branding. They knew his books from cover to cover, knew of him and his many talents, and he did not leave the book festival with a single book. He had to send a fan to his room to get the remaining books he'd brought with him. His genre is fiction and he is a master storyteller who is literally in love with his characters. He spoke of them as if they were family members and I felt like I was at one big family reunion and I'd never read one of his books, ever. I left with a passion to have more readers hunger for the words I write like that. Let's call it professional jealousy with a healthy dose of gratitude for the experience that made me want to expand my territory.

Another major social media phenomenon is "live streaming." Facebook, Instagram, and YouTube are all major social media platforms which support this instantaneous "in your face" viewing platform. As an author mastering live streaming is a great way to get in touch with your viewers and "expand your territory."

For more information on the "how to" aspects of live streaming check out kimgarst.com. She has been instrumental in helping thousands of business owners (authors included) build and grow their businesses.

This chapter is an instrument if used correctly it will generate you many happy moments and memories. For some of you, it will take a leap of faith to leave the chair that is positioned securely behind your iPad or PC. Trust me if you allow yourself to venture into the unfamiliar land of branding yourself and your book, you will not only expand your territory but you will learn to enjoy the celebrated beauty and essence of who you are as a writer. After all it's all about you. Happy Writing!

Summary

One of my favorite books as a child was *The Little Engine that Could*, by Arnold Munk. I was an introverted skinny kid with thick glasses not athletically inclined and scared of new experiences. My only claim to fame was my ability to write and read profusely. I would read this particular book to gain courage to do the things normal kids did without thinking about it such as crossing a crowded street, reciting a poem in a church play, or approaching someone to be my friend. I take this trip down memory lane to encourage you to hold tight to your "bestseller" dream.

Your daily confession as an aspiring best-selling author should be: "I-think-I-can! I-think-I- can! I-think-I-can! ..." and you will! With patience and perseverance, you will be saying, just like the little engine: "I-thought-I-could! I-thought-I-could!

I-thought-I-could!" The purpose of this chapter is to encourage you to dream big dreams for your book project. I believe with hard work and a little divine intervention you can accomplish anything. Happy Writing!

CHAPTER ELEVEN

IT'S ALL ABOUT GOD'S WILL

ഇൻൽ

The book of Nehemiah is a shining example of bravery, unwavering commitment and love for God. Nehemiah was a mere man who embraced His God with unquestionable faith. He modeled the warrior spirit of King David when he strategized to defeat the plans of his enemies for his failure. He modeled the wisdom of Solomon when he developed a plan not only to build the wall of Jerusalem but to restore Judah to its original glory. He modeled an unquenchable love for God when He was moved like Jesus Christ with compassion for his people. Nehemiah laid the spiritual foundation for 21st Century Christian Authorpreneurs. 21st Century Christian Authorpreneurs evaluate their progress.

Leaving a Lasting Testimony

Charting your progress by doing periodic evaluations and maintenance on the completed work is crucial to your continued success. Nehemiah returned to check on the progress of Jerusalem after the wall was built. (Nehemiah 13:6). It wasn't quite what he expected when he arrived. The people had returned to some of their old wrong ways. He had a cushy job in Persia, Nehemiah could have easily spent the rest of his life there, but his love for God and his people made him concerned for their wellbeing, so he returned to Jerusalem to evaluate his God project.

Now that you know your "who," "what," "when," "where," and "why," it's time to implement your plan of action, you are officially an authorpreneur adequately equipped for your literary journey. Don't sit back and enjoy the ride just yet. You've laid out an excellent plan for your journey now you only have to stop occasionally for gas and to do regularly scheduled maintenance. The regularly scheduled maintenance is called evaluation. An evaluation plan is the tool you used to perform that appraisal. Earlier, you established goals and objectives. You determined:

a. If your book was sellable by looking at the current market in your genre.

b. If the market is large enough for you to join the party.

c. A niche or problem not being addressed in your genre you could address.

d. If you have the right stuff, education and/or experience comparable to other authors in your genre and how to better posture yourself for success in that genre.

e. The needs of your target market and design a plan to meet those needs.

f. When is the best time to launch your book?

g. What is the best marketing strategy for you prior to the book launch and afterwards.

h. What type of publishing best fits your needs?

So take a moment and give yourself a hand for being a great student. You get an A+ for all your hard work and diligence. Now, let's see how well you play with others. You and your advisory team determine how regularly an appraisal is required. I recommend you establish a timeline to monitor your progress daily if you are a beginner to this process. A timeline acts as a guide which equips you to stay focused on your objectives. You could use a standard paper, electronic calendar, a timeline template, or get an app which sends you reminders from your smart phone. There are numerous methods you can use. The method you choose should be easily accessible, visible and user friendly.

Now it's time to revisit your mission. Is your project financially driven or message driven? If your goal is to sell a certain number of books by a certain time, your evaluation plan will be centered on meeting that objective. Some of the things you may want to consider are: How many books do you want to sell weekly or monthly? Which method will best help you keep track of your progress? What cost effective tool can you use to measure the results you are generating? Will you use a POD (Print-On-Demand) publisher or rely on a traditional publisher for book distribution?

You can answer these questions by identifying specific events or initiatives you have designed which support your goals and objective for your book project and chart their success. If they work keep them in the plan.

If your goal is message driven, your evaluation plan will be based on the number of individuals who are reached with that message. Keep abreast of local, regional, and national opportunities which align with your book's premise or subject matter with special occasions, national observances, or current events and make sure you contribute your voice by providing a commentary as an expert and don't forget to mention your book in the process.

Keep track of the outcomes from your marketing efforts and drive readers to your website, Facebook page, or blog. You may want to use Google Analytics to keep track of your marketing ROI (Return On Investment) on your electronic media.

Evaluating Your Team

Periodically it's a good thing to get feedback from your team on how you are doing and how they feel the book process is moving forward. I have included a great tool for them to evaluate their contribution and the progress of the project below.

BOOK PROJECT TEAM EVALUATION

Directions: On a scale of 1 – 10 (1 being the lowest and 10 being the highest), rank each statement based on your observation as a team member.

1. The team has full and common understanding of the roles and responsibilities of the team._

2. The team understands the author's mission and vision for their products and services.

3. The structural purpose of every support team member is clear.

4. The team has clear goals and actions resulting from relevant and realistic strategic planning.

5. The team gives regular status reports on finances/budgets, products/project performance and other important matters.

6. The team helps set book project goals and is actively involved in the project.

7. The team effectively supports the author in book related events.

8. Team meetings facilitate focus and progress on important matters relating to the book project.

9. The team regularly monitors and evaluates progress toward strategic goals and product/ project performance.

10. Each member of the team feels involved and interested in the team's work.

11. All necessary skills, talents, and professional needs are represented in the team for book project success.

Please list the three to five points on which you believe the team should focus its attention in the next quarter. Be as specific as possible in identifying these points.

1.

2.

3.

4.

Select an evaluation method which best fits your publishing personality and religiously keep track of your progress. We've had fun traveling with you on this journey to AUTHORSHIP, we've even taken over the wheel sometimes but now you have enough tools to finish this journey on your own. Happy Evaluating!!!

When Nehemiah returned to Jerusalem, he confronted the problems of the people head on and corrected their actions and put them back on the path to honoring God and keeping His commandments. Now is the time to ask yourself, are you a present day Nehemiah? Has He called you to address the things in the world that aren't right? If so that can be a little scary.

I sought the LORD, and he answered me; he delivered me from all my fears. Psalm 34:4

The million-dollar question is where do we fit in a lost and dying world? It's frightening to consider the plight of the modern day Christian. As the days get darker and the hearts of men are being hardened towards God there is a clarion call for the believer to assume the position of an evangelist. Is Christ not the answer for the ills of this world? Do we not serve a risen Savior who is seated at the right hand of the Father interceding for us? Can we not find what we need in Him to win this battle of good versus evil that confronts us daily? Jesus showed us how to be victorious in all we are called to do for His kingdom. Will we trust Him?

Our times are not unlike those Nehemiah lived in. Accepting the call of the scribe can be intimidating. We look at our laptops and tablets and say, "Me, Lord? You've called me to fulfill The Great Commission with my pen?" If you are now asking yourself that question then seek the face of God for His answer and be prepared for His response. Sometimes it's scary even asking the question because we really don't want to hear the answer. It may require a sacrifice ...

In order to save his people from utter destruction, Nehemiah was required to leave all he was familiar with and return to his homeland. When he arrived, it held no resemblance to what he remembered as a boy or to the stories his ancestors shared with him about the good old days but he knew His God and what He was capable of doing and he trusted Him to do it. He had an overwhelming confidence in God to perform His will regardless of the situation or circumstance. Nehemiah had uncompromising faith!

Do you have uncompromising faith? Abraham, Isaac, Jacob, Moses, David, Esther, Ruth, Mary Paul, Peter, Mark, and Matthew, all ordinary people with an extraordinary faith. How do you differ from them? The Bible does an excellent job of showing us their successes and failures. They were mere humans doing things considered impossible for common man but when you put God in the equation all things become possible.

The book of Nehemiah is also a living testament to the faithfulness of God. He not only said He would restore His people but He strategically brought it to past in His due season. Perhaps God is calling you to play a major role in restoring His people to their rightful place in Him in the land you live in or to another place for a season until His will is fulfilled. Whatever God has purposed for you to do as a Christian Authorpreneur, He needs you to show up for duty, now. You cannot live in the world we live in and not be aware of the need for God's love. We have reached an era where the only church some people will experience is that which they are exposed to in the pages of a book you write. What if you didn't write it? What if you wrote it and didn't publish it? What if you published it and didn't market it and the message didn't get to the people group who needed it so desperately? What if you decide like the rich young ruler, your wealth was more important than serving God and being used to fulfill His purpose on the earth?

These are all valid questions practicing Christians should ask themselves before they venture to write. Being an author requires courage and being a Christian Authorpreneur requires love. We need to be so much in love with God, our fellow brothers and sisters in the Lord, and ourselves we become infectious enough to change the world around us. Wow! We get to do that from behind our laptops and tablets. We get to love others into the Kingdom of God through the messages we share with the world. I think it's time for a celebration. Nehemiah and the children of Israel celebrated when the wall was finished. We get to attend because a scribe chronicled this grand event. Nehemiah 12:27 – 43 tells the whole story:

> At the dedication of the wall of Jerusalem, the Levites were sought out from where they lived and were brought to Jerusalem to celebrate joyfully the dedication with songs of thanksgiving and with the music of cymbals, harps and lyres. The musicians also were brought together from the region around Jerusalem—from the villages of the Netophathites, from Beth Gilgal, and from the area of Geba and Azmaveth, for the musicians had built villages for themselves around Jerusalem. When the priests and Levites had purified themselves ceremonially, they purified the people, the gates and the wall.
>
> I had the leaders of Judah go up on top of the wall. I also assigned two large choirs to give thanks. One was to proceed on top off the wall to the right, toward the Dung Gate. Hoshaiah and half the leaders of Judah followed them, along with Azariah, Ezra, Meshullam, Judah, Benjamin, Shemaiah, Jeremiah, as well as some priests with trumpets, and also Zechariah son of Jonathan, the son of Shemaiah, the son of

Mattaniah, the son of Micaiah, the son of Zakkur, the son of Asaph, and his associates—Shemaiah, Azarel, Milalai, Gilalai, Maai, Nethanel, Judah and Hanani—with musical instruments prescribed by David the man of God. Ezra the teacher of the Law led the procession. At the Fountain Gate they continued directly up the steps of the City of David on the ascent to the wall and passed above the site of David's palace to the Water Gate on the east.

The second choir proceeded in the opposite direction. I followed them on top of the wall, together with half the people—past the Tower of the Ovens to the Broad Wall, over the Gate of Ephraim, the Jeshanahh Gate, the Fish Gate, the Tower of Hananel and the Tower of the Hundred, as far as the Sheep Gate. At the Gate of the Guard they stopped.

The two choirs that gave thanks then took their places in the house of God; so did I, together with half the officials, as well as the priests—Eliakim, Maaseiah, Miniamin, Micaiah, Elioenai, Zechariah and Hananiah with their trumpets—and also Maaseiah, Shemaiah, Eleazar, Uzzi, Jehohanan, Malkijah, Elam and Ezer. The choirs sang under the direction of Jezrahiah. And on that day they offered great sacrifices, rejoicing because God had given them great joy. The women and children also rejoiced. The sound of rejoicing in Jerusalem could be heard far away.

What a testimony to God's goodness! Speaking of goodness, it was Nehemiah's desire he be remembered for the good he'd done in Jerusalem. (Nehemiah 13:31) Do you want God to remember you for the good you've done? It may not be a popular stance but it's a very rewarding one. Just ask Nehemiah, I hear God's benefit package is heavenly. Happy Writing!

Prayer for Your Book Project©

☙☙

Lord we come in the name higher than every name, Jesus Christ, lifting up Your call on my life to write a book. We dedicate all that is to take place to You and pray our work continuously brings glory to Your kingdom. Let the hands of all You have assigned to this project be anointed to declare and perform great and mighty works. May the words of our hearts and the meditation of our minds be consistently saturated in Your word, that we may adequately express Your truth. May You, Jehovah Jireh, be our consistent provider and make supernatural provision available as we move forward in faith for the success of this book project.

I decree and declare that our hearts have been stirred by your righteous cause and our hands have been surrendered to the King of Kings so we may do an excellent work. Our purpose is to write the true revelatory word of God, that the hearts of the people may rejoice and their joy would be complete in you. Bringing honor to Jesus, who purposely determines to write his love eternally upon their hearts. He is the master author who has entrusted us with the responsibility of etching a lasting testimony of God's love for all mankind. We will publish the name of the Lord, for He is great and greatly to be praised.

As you commanded the Apostle John, so have I written in this book the revelatory word of God. Enable me to continue to seek your wisdom and counsel concerning this book. Give me understanding and discernment as I prepare to launch this book into the universe. Reveal to me any hidden costs or expenses, so I can take them into account as I develop an accurate budget for the launch of this book. Give everyone involved in this project the ability to concentrate their attention and efforts so they can successfully complete this undertaking and thereby bring honor and glory to You. [1]

Father, make Your face to shine upon me and enlighten me as I seek You first so that the success of this launch may be added unto me. I declare no weapon formed against this book project shall prosper and every tongue that rises against it will be shown to be in the wrong because this is a God idea wrapped in Your purpose. Bring me to find favor, compassion, and loving kindness with reviewers, vendors, media partners, business partners, marketing and public relations specialists and potential readers.

Thank You Father that I am even now increasing in favor with You and with man. May the works of my hands continue to exalt, edify, equip, and exhort Your people. We thank You for the completed work done by Jesus Christ on Calvary through His blood which covers this book and we thank You in advance

---

1   Modified from Prayers That Avail Much for the Workplace, Germaine Copeland

for the completed successful work done through my efforts to build Your kingdom. In Jesus' name, we pray. Amen.

ABOUT THE AUTHOR

ΣΟ

Authorpreneurs are a rare breed. They authentically combine two skill sets, writing, and entrepreneurship, to create a space in the literary marketplace for their creativity." Sharon C. Jenkins

Sharon C. Jenkins is the Inspirational Principal for The Master Communicator's Writing Services. Her business provides writing and coaching services to small businesses, nonprofits, and authors. Known as The Master Communicator, she has mastered multiple forms of media communications in writing, publishing, and speaking. Her professional experience ranges from working as an editor for a major, minority-owned communications and marketing company to being a senior publishing consultant for an award-winning publishing house. She is a best-selling and award-winning author. Her expertise includes business communications, entrepreneurship, book coaching, publishing, and marketing. She is affectionately known as a "literary midwife" and has helped hundreds of authors "birth" their book babies.

She started her journey as a poet, graduated to a playwright, and is now an award-winning, Amazon bestselling author, blogger, and podcaster. Her solo projects consists of the following titles: Beyond the Closet Door, Christ's Rescue from Abuse, Authorpreneurship: The Business Start-Up Manual for Authors, and The Super Author Journal, The Super Authordom Notebook, and a host of e-books tailored for authors on such topics as writing, marketing, time management, and publishing.

Her most recent print releases for authors are compilations titled, Are you a Super Author? and You Can Be a Super Author Too! These books have "How to Get It Done" stories of seasoned authorpreneurs loaded with the hiccups and tips from their journey. They were intentionally designed to be a literary inspiration for authors interested in starting a business in writing.

Sharon has been a featured blogger on Huffington Post, The Good Men Project, Self-Published Author, Afrovibesradio.com, and Book Marketing Tools. She also hosts her podcast Luminance (available on most podcast platforms) where she sheds the light on people who are doing good in the world. Sharon is also a board member of the award-winning Brilliant Women in Film, whose creative team directed and produced her mini documentary, The Birthing of a Book Baby. She has been the conference host for multiple writers' conferences around the nation. She has also been a featured panelist or speaker at national, regional, and local events such as the national NAACP and Urban League conferences, WriterCon, the Authors Marketing Guild, Houston's Writefest, Living Your Dreams Conference, the Marketplace Fair's Author Showcase, Houston Independent Authors' Writers Lunch, Nonfiction Authors Association, and the Houston

Writers Guild. For more information about Sharon go to www. supersuthorgranny.com or www.mcwritingservices.com.

◈ Here's her reasons for the love and devotion she has for authors: Authors are stars because they light up a room with their intellectual brilliance

◈ Authors uphold the lead because they are trailblazers, dreamers, and innovators creating new paradigm shifts in the thinking and emotional responses of their readers.

◈ Authors are truly superheroes because they "dare to go where no man has gone before," and write their way into the hearts and minds of their unsuspecting audience without speaking a single word. Now that's powerful!

COMING SOON...
THE UNTOLD LOVE STORY
BY SHARON C. JENKINS

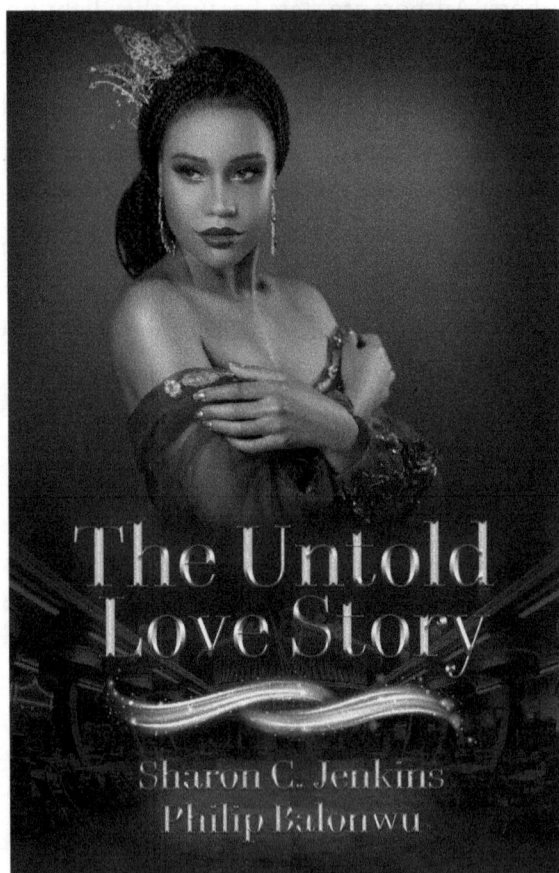

The Untold
Love Story

Sharon C. Jenkins
Philip Balonwu

JUST IN TIME FOR THE NEW YEAR!
Go to www.superauthorgranny.com for more information.